Laboratory Manual:
the
PHYSICAL WORLD
An Introduction to Physical Science
for Christian Schools

Thomas G. Lamb

R. Terrance Egolf

Linda E. Shumate

Bob Jones University Press • Greenville, South Carolina 29614

The authors and the publisher have made every effort to ensure that the investigations and demonstrations in this publication are safe when conducted according to the instructions provided. We assume no responsibility for any injury or damage caused or sustained while performing the activities in this book. Conventional/home school teachers, parents, and guardians should closely supervise students who perform the investigations in this manual. More specific safety information is contained in the Teacher's Edition of *The Physical World: An Introduction to Physical Science Laboratory Manual* published by Bob Jones University Press. Therefore, it is strongly recommended that the Teacher's Edition be used in conjunction with this manual.

Note:
The fact that materials produced by other publishers may be referred to in this volume does not constitute an endorsement of the content or theological position of materials produced by such publishers. Any references and ancillary materials are listed as an aid to the student or the teacher and in an attempt to maintain the accepted academic standards of the publishing industry.

Laboratory Manual:
THE PHYSICAL WORLD
AN INTRODUCTION TO PHYSICAL SCIENCE for Christian Schools®

Thomas Lamb, Ph.D.
R. Terrance Egolf, CDR, USN (Ret.)
Linda Shumate

Cover Design
Jeremy Jantz

Cover Photo: PhotoDisc, Inc.

Produced in cooperation with the Division of Natural Science
of the Bob Jones University College of Arts and Science.

for Christian Schools is a registered trademark of Bob Jones University Press.

©2001 Bob Jones University Press
Greenville, South Carolina 29614

Printed in the United States of America
All rights reserved

ISBN 1-57924-418-1

20 19 18 17 16 15 14 13 12 11 10 9 8 7 6 5 4

CONTENTS

Introduction   v

Chapter One: Science and the Christian
  1A Investigation: Laboratory Safety   1
  1B Investigation: Observations and Classification   7

Chapter Two: The Scientific Method
  2A Investigation: Scientific Method   15
  2B Investigation: Scientific Reports   21

Chapter Three: The Measurement of Matter
  3A Applications: Significant Digits/Reading Scales   27
  3B Applications: Significant Digits in Calculations   33
  3C Investigation: Measuring   39
  3D Investigation: Density   45

Chapter Four: The Properties of Matter
  4A Investigation: Chemical and Physical Changes   53
  4B Investigation: Finding Absolute Zero   59

Chapter Five: The Classification of Matter
  5A Teacher Demonstration: Elements   65
  5B Teacher Demonstration: Compounds   71
  5C Investigation: Mixtures   75

Chapter Six: Models of Atoms
  6A Teacher Demonstration: Flame Tests   79
  6B Investigation: Radioactive Decay   83

Chapter Seven: The Periodic Table of Elements
  7   Investigation: Metals and Nonmetals   89

Chapter Eight: Forces Between Atoms
  8A Applications: Ionic Bonding   95
  8B Applications: Covalent Bonding   97
  8C Applications: Bonding Summary   101
  8D Investigation: Identifying Bond Types   103

Chapter Nine: Chemical Reactions
  9A Applications: Chemical Formulas   109
  9B Applications: Chemical Equations   113
  9C Teacher Demonstration: Chemical Reactions   117

Chapter Ten: Solutions
  10 Investigation: Phase Changes in Solutions   123

Chapter Eleven: Acids, Bases, and Salts
  11 Investigation: pH of Common Solutions   129

Chapter Twelve: Energy and Momentum

12   Applications: Stopping Distances 135

Chapter Thirteen: Mechanics: Matter in Motion

13A Applications: Yellow Light: Stop or Go? 141

13B Investigation: Center of Gravity 147

Chapter Fourteen: Work and Machines

14A Investigation: First-Class Levers 155

14B Investigation: Second- and Third-Class Levers 163

14C Investigation: Inclined Planes 173

Chapter Fifteen: Fluid Mechanics

15A Teacher Demonstration: Pressure 181

15B Investigation: Buoyancy 189

15C Applications: Boyle's and Charles's Laws 193

Chapter Sixteen: Heat and Temperature

16A Teacher Demonstration: Temperature, Heat, and Thermal Energy   199

16B Investigation: Specific Heat 205

Chapter Seventeen: Electricity

17A Investigation: Static Electricity 211

17B Investigation: Circuits 219

Chapter Eighteen: Magnetism

18A Investigation: Magnetic Fields: Bar Magnets 233

18B Investigation: Electromagnets 241

Chapter Nineteen: Sound Waves

19A Teacher Demonstration: Waves 249

19B Teacher Demonstration: Properties of Sound 255

Chapter Twenty: The Electromagnetic Spectrum

20A Teacher Demonstration: Wave Properties 259

20B Investigation: Virtual Images 267

20C Investigation: Lenses 271

INTRODUCTION

If science were merely a collection of facts, you would need only an encyclopedia to study science. You could simply research, read, and memorize information that someone else had collected. But science is much more than just a collection of facts. It is a working process, a method of thinking, and a way to solve problems. Science is what scientists do; memorizing a textbook full of facts could not teach you true science.

When it comes to learning, nothing can compare to hands-on experience. The investigations and demonstrations in this book were developed so that you will become genuinely interested in science. Through attention to detail, hard work, and good old-fashioned persistence, you will earn a great appreciation for scientific research and how valuable it is to our present understanding of the physical world.

Purposes

This laboratory manual was developed for the following purposes:

- *To help you understand how science works.* Science is a method of gathering information and solving problems that relate to the physical universe. You will not *imitate* scientists in this course; you will actually *be* a scientist. You will see firsthand how science works, what it can do, and what it cannot do.

- *To help you remember the information in your textbook.* You can remember information more easily when you use it than when you simply memorize it. The applications, investigations, and demonstrations in this laboratory manual allow you to review, apply, and observe the ideas you have encountered in your textbook.

- *To help you develop scientific attitudes.* Are you curious? Do you make decisions based on facts? How do you react when some fact seems to contradict one of your beliefs? A scientific attitude will help you make reasonable decisions in areas as different as buying clothes, forming opinions about ecology, and choosing which courses to take in school.

- *To help you build problem-solving skills.* All your life you will be solving some sort of problem. This laboratory manual will guide you in making accurate observations and sound judgments as you investigate scientific problems.

- *To help you learn laboratory skills.* The activities in this manual will teach you to make accurate measurements and to use common laboratory equipment safely.

Procedures

No book can force you to learn. You are responsible for the benefit you gain from each class period. With the proper attitude and consistent effort, you can succeed. In order to do your best work, follow these procedures as you use this book.

- *Before each class period*

1. Read the entire exercise that your teacher has assigned. Answer the pre-laboratory questions. If you do this, you will be more efficient during lab time because you will know what you are supposed to be doing.

2. Review the textbook material that matches the topic of the investigation. You cannot benefit from an activity if you do not understand what principles it is supposed to teach you.

3. Plan ahead. Organize your work so that you can complete each investigation quickly and efficiently.

4. Bring all necessary supplies with you to class. Besides your lab manual, you will need your textbook, extra paper, and pencils with erasers. For some investigations you may want to bring an apron or an old shirt to protect your school clothes.

- *During the class period*

1. Follow carefully all the instructions given by your teacher as well as all the instructions in your laboratory manual. Do not proceed with the investigation until told to do so.

2. Work efficiently. Restrict your talking to questions that will help you do your work better.

3. Ask questions if you are not sure what to do. The time you spend getting your questions answered will be far less than the time you spend hesitating to begin because of confusion.

4. Record your results accurately. Observations should be recorded as soon as possible after they are made. You may postpone answering some of the questions in the investigation until after class in order to save time.

5. Put each piece of equipment away and clean up your work area when you have completed the investigation.

- *After the class period*

1. Answer all the questions in the investigation. Because the first and most important step to a good grade is completeness, you should do your own work. Although the observations you make will often be the same as your partner's, never copy answers to questions.

2. Answer the questions whenever possible in complete, thoughtful statements. Try to explain why your answer is true using the concepts you have learned.

3. Promptly turn in your report to your teacher.

4. File your work in a three-ring notebook after your teacher has returned it.

Policies

When you walk into a laboratory, you are walking into a potentially dangerous place. What may seem like innocent horseplay could end up seriously hurting you or your classmates or damaging expensive equipment. Obey the following rules and any other guidelines your teacher sets up for your laboratory.

1. Follow closely all written instructions and listen carefully when your teacher gives you instructions.

2. Never perform unauthorized experiments. It is good to be curious, but you should never mix chemicals together to "see what will happen."

3. Wear safety goggles and protective clothing whenever you use chemicals or a heat source.

4. Know where eyewashes, fire blankets, emergency showers, and fire extinguishers are located. Learn how to use them.

5. Avoid touching chemicals. Never taste chemicals or let them touch your eyes. Smell chemicals by fanning their vapors toward your nose with your hand. Never smell chemicals by inhaling deeply.

6. Secure long hair and loose clothing that could interfere with your work.

7. Never heat a closed container. When heating a test tube, flask, or beaker, point the open end away from yourself and any other people in the room.

8. Keep your workspaces neat and uncluttered.

9. Report any accident, however minor it may seem, to the teacher.

10. Keep combustible materials away from open flames.

11. With large amounts of water flush any acids or bases that are spilled on clothing or skin .

We hope that you will have a safe and exciting year studying science, one that will provide you with valuable information and experience. This lab manual will help you to achieve goals that you have set for yourself, but more importantly, it will open doors for you into areas of science you may not have known existed. Even if you don't enter into a career in science, you will undoubtedly face many situations in life in which a basic knowledge of science is crucial. This is the time of your life where you should be walking through open doors, not slamming them shut before you look inside. Who knows—once you walk through the door, you may like what you see!

1A **INVESTIGATION**

Laboratory Safety

Name _Brooke Cary_

Date _9/22/08_ Hour _12:20 pm_

Objectives

The purpose of this exercise is to

1. Familiarize you with the basic rules for laboratory safety.

2. Point out safety equipment in the laboratory.

3. Review basic first aid for common accidents.

4. Identify information on warning labels of common products.

5. Discuss the personal protection and hazard index.

Materials List

Suggested household products

Bleach

Hair spray

Household cleaner

Shaving cream

Paint

Suggested laboratory chemicals

Sodium fluoride

Ammonium nitrate

Mercuric chloride

Lead metal

Introduction

The laboratories that you will perform in this course have been designed with the maximum safety possible. However, even household items can become dangerous if they are not used properly. Before you begin a laboratory investigation, you are expected to have read and understood the procedures. You may not begin the in-class portion of the investigation until directed to do so by your teacher. These rules are for your safety, so follow them at all times.

Pre-Laboratory Questions

Read the entire investigation. Answer the following questions prior to class on a separate sheet of paper. Use complete sentences.

1. What is the purpose of this investigation?

2. What should you do if a chemical splashes in your eye?

3. Can household products be dangerous? How can you tell?

4. Give the four items that a label on a container should contain.

5. Give two reasons that household and laboratory chemicals should be stored only in their designated containers.

Basic Laboratory Rules

1. Never perform any experiment without the teacher's permission.
2. Avoid playful, distracting, or boisterous behavior.
3. Work at your own station and do not "visit" with other groups.
4. Never have food or drink in a laboratory.
5. Never taste any chemicals or drink out of any chemical glassware.
6. Place solid trash in the wastebasket and liquid wastes in designated containers.
7. Notify the teacher of any injuries, spills, or breakages.
8. Never leave a flame or heater unattended.

Laboratory Safety Features

A. Eyewash stations (if equipped)
   1. The purpose of the eyewash station is to remove any chemical that gets into your eyes.
   2. Locate the eyewash stations in the room and turn on the water to see how the stations work.

B. Showers (if equipped)
   1. The purpose of the showers is to wash any dangerous chemicals off your clothes or skin.
   2. Locate the shower in the laboratory and observe how it works. **Do not test the shower.**

C. Fire blanket (if equipped)
   1. The purpose of the fire blanket is to wrap up a person if his clothes catch fire.
   2. Locate the fire blanket in the room.

D. Fire extinguishers
1. There may be several different types of fire extinguishers available that are made for different types of fires.

2. Locate the fire extinguishers and determine their specific use.

              Location   *Use*

     a. _____   _____

     b. _____   _____

Basic First Aid for Minor Injuries (Notify the lab instructor of all accidents.)

1. Eyes—If any chemical gets into your eyes, remove contact lenses and flush the area with plenty of water for fifteen minutes. Seek medical attention.

2. Minor heat burns—Apply cold water to the affected area.

3. Acid or alkali burns—Flush the area with plenty of water. If irritation persists, seek medical attention.

4. Cuts—Wash the area thoroughly with soap and water.

5. Inhalation of chemical dust or vapors—Remove to fresh air and observe for ten to fifteen minutes. Seek medical attention if breathing distress continues.

Warning Labels

Laboratory chemicals and common household products can be dangerous if they are not used properly. Labels on the containers should specify the hazards, first aid procedures, personal protection information, and the hazard index. Complete the following information about the following chemicals. It may not be possible to complete the information on every product since the labels may not contain all of the information. This investigation can be completed by using products found at home.

1. Hazard index
     Health (e.g., 3—serious hazard)
     Flammability
     Reactivity

2. Personal protection index (e.g., D—face shield, gloves, synthetic apron)

3. Warnings—Warnings may include the following:
     Target organs
     Combustible or explosive
     Strong oxidizer or corrosive
     Storage and disposal instructions

4. First aid

5. Use

A. *Bleach*

1. Hazard index—Health _____   Flammability _____   Reactivity _____

2. Personal protection _____

3. Warnings _____

    _____

    a. The target organs: _____, _____, and _____

    b. Bleach cannot be used with what? _____

    _____

    c. What happens if bleach is used with these products? _____

    _____

    d. What will bleach do to metals? _____

    e. Storage or disposal instructions _____

    _____

4. First Aid—

    a. _____

    b. _____

    c. _____

5. Use _____

B. _____ (Chemical)

1. Hazard index—Health _____   Flammability _____   Reactivity _____

2. Personal protection _____

3. Warnings _____

    _____

    Target organs _____, _____, and _____

    Storage or disposal instructions _____

4. First aid

    _____

    _____

    _____

5. Use _____

C. _____ (Chemical)

   1. Hazard index—Health _____   Flammability _____   Reactivity _____

   2. Personal protection _____

   3. Warnings _____

       _____

       Target organs _____, _____, and _____

       Storage or disposal instructions _____

   4. First aid

       _____

       _____

       _____

   5. Use _____

D. _____ (Chemical)

   1. Hazard index—Health _____   Flammability _____   Reactivity _____

   2. Personal protection _____

   3. Warnings _____

       _____

       Target organs _____, _____, and _____

       Storage or disposal instructions _____

   4. First aid

       _____

       _____

       _____

   5. Use _____

E. _____ (Chemical)

   1. Hazard index—Health _____   Flammability _____   Reactivity _____

   2. Personal protection _____

   3. Warnings _____

       _____

       Target organs _____, _____, and _____

       Storage or disposal instructions _____

   4. First aid

       _____

       _____

       _____

   5. Use _____

F. _____ (Chemical)

  1. Hazard index—Health _____   Flammability _____   Reactivity _____

  2. Personal protection _____

  3. Warnings _____

    _____

    Target organs _____, _____, and _____

    Storage or disposal instructions _____

  4. First aid

    _____

    _____

    _____

  5. Use _____

G. (Optional) _____ (Chemical)

  1. Hazard index—Health _____   Flammability _____   Reactivity _____

  2. Personal protection _____

  3. Warnings _____

    _____

    Target organs _____, _____, and _____

    Storage or disposal instructions _____

  4. First aid

    _____

    _____

    _____

  5. Use _____

H. (Optional) _____ (Chemical)

  1. Hazard index—Health _____   Flammability _____   Reactivity _____

  2. Personal protection _____

  3. Warnings _____

    _____

    Target organs _____, _____, and _____

    Storage or disposal instructions _____

  4. First aid

    _____

    _____

    _____

  5. Use _____

1B INVESTIGATION

Observations and Classification

Name _____

Date _____ Hour_____

Objectives

The purpose of this investigation is to touch you to make objective observations about common items and then to use those observations to classify the items into groups.

Materials

Apple juice
Cola
Cold water
Paper
Penny
Pepper
Rock
Table salt
Wooden block

Equipment

Beaker (250 mL)
Metric ruler
Thermometer

Introduction

A good scientist must make careful and accurate observations so that other scientists can **replicate** (reproduce in a similar way) the results of experiments. To make these observations, the scientist uses his senses. To make the observations more precise, instruments are frequently used. Instruments also make observations more **objective.** An objective observation is one that results from a measurement or the use of descriptive terms that are well defined. **Subjective** observations have limited usefulness in science since they include the observer's personal opinion or use terms that are **ambiguous** (lack precise meaning). For example, a person from Mexico may say that the weather outside is cool, whereas, an Eskimo may say that the weather is warm. These subjective observations can be made objective by stating that the temperature is 65° F. By stating the degrees, personal opinion and ambiguity are avoided.

Scientists do not just make observations. They use these observations to classify data, formulate questions, evaluate ideas, and test theories. The facts or data recorded in observations cannot change, but as scientists identify new information, the interpretations of those facts change, leading to new scientific theories. Scientific principles are continually being modified and retested by different experiments.

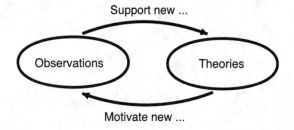

Pre-Laboratory Questions

Read the entire investigation. Answer the following questions prior to class on a separate sheet of paper. Use complete sentences.

1. Define the following terms.
   a. Replicate
   b. Objective
   c. Subjective
   d. Ambiguous

2. What about science does not change, and what about science is always changing?

Observation Exercise

Selected objects will be given to you for this exercise. For each object, you must write the most accurate descriptive term for each attribute listed on the form that follows. Your teacher may provide suggested descriptions for some of the categories. Some attributes may not be applicable (e.g., flexibility for a liquid). A wooden block will be done as a class example.

Wooden Block

State (solid, liquid, gas)	Odor
Shape	Texture
Size	Hardness
Color	Other observations
Temperature	
Flexibility	

Subjective terms that are very general should be avoided in scientific descriptions whenever possible. To help you distinguish the difference between subjective and objective terms, write a subjective description of the wooden block in the blanks on the next page.

Wooden Block (Subjective description)

Size

Temperature

Hardness

Rock

State (solid, liquid, gas)	Odor
Shape	Texture
Size	Hardness
Color	Other observatioins
Temperature	
Flexibility	

Cold Water

State (solid, liquid, gas)	Odor
Shape	Texture
Size	Hardness
Color	Other observations
Temperature	
Flexibility	

Cola

State (solid, liquid, gas)	Odor
Shape	Texture
Size	Hardness
Color	Other observations
Temperature	
Flexibility	

Air

State (solid, liquid, gas)	Odor
Shape	Texture
Size	Hardness
Color	Other observations
Temperature	
Flexibility	

Paper

State (solid, liquid, gas)	Odor
Shape	Texture
Size	Hardness
Color	Other observations
Temperature	
Flexibility	

Table Salt

State (solid, liquid, gas)	Odor
Shape	Texture
Size	Hardness
Color	Other observations
Temperature	
Flexibility	

Pepper

State (solid, liquid, gas)	Odor
Shape	Texture
Size	Hardness
Color	Other observations
Temperature	
Flexibility	

Apple Juice

State (solid, liquid, gas)	Odor
Shape	Texture
Size	Hardness
Color	Other observations
Temperature	
Flexibility	

Penny

State (solid, liquid, gas)	Odor
Shape	Texture
Size	Hardness
Color	Other observations
Temperature	
Flexibility	

_____ **(Optional)**

State (solid, liquid, gas)	Odor
Shape	Texture
Size	Hardness
Color	Other observations
Temperature	
Flexibility	

Classification Exercise

A collection of observations has little scientific value by itself. The scientist must give meaning to the facts by making an **inference,** that is, deducing something or drawing as a conclusion some new idea. For example, atmospheric information obtained from radar is not useful until a weather forecaster interprets the data and predicts the weather. One way of making an inference is **classification.** To classify means to separate objects into groups that are based on a common characteristic. Establishing a rule based on observable features allows you to make up groups. An example of a rule based on a physical feature would be the color of the object. A rule based upon usefulness would be suitability for a particular use, such as starting a fire.

In this exercise you will classify the observed objects by first establishing a rule. The rule will define two or more different groups in such a way that all objects will fit in one of the groups. The objects in each group will be listed. The objects will be classified two different ways based upon physical characteristics. Do not use the rule given in the example.

Example

Objects observed: wooden block, paper, rock, cold water, table salt, cola, air, pepper, apple juice, penny

	Rule	**Objects**
Group 1	White objects	Table salt, paper
Group 2	Non-white objects	Wooden block, rock, cold water, cola, air, pepper, apple juice, penny

Classification 1 (Physical characteristic) _____
List all the objects that you observed.

	Rule	**Objects**
Group 1		
Group 2		

Classification 2 (Physical characteristic) _____
List all the objects that you observed.

	Rule	**Objects**
Group 1		
Group 2		

Classification 3 (Optional—Usefulness) _____
List all the objects that you observed.

	Rule	**Objects**
Group 1		
Group 2		

Discussion Questions

1. Define the following terms.

   Inference _____

   _____

   Classification _____

   _____

2. Change the following subjective observations into objective statements.

Subjective	Objective
a. Hot	a. _____
b. Cold	b. _____
c. Long	c. _____
d. Heavy	d. _____
e. Colorful	e. _____

3. Why are inferences necessary in science? _____

_____

4. Do you think that all objects in nature will neatly fit into the classification systems devised by scientists? Explain your answer. _____

_____

_____

5. Scientists use their _____ to obtain observations, and _____ are used to make their observations more precise and less biased.

6. An objective observation is one that can be _____ by another scientist.

7. Why is replication important in science? _____

_____

_____

Observations and Classification

Name _____

Date _____ Hour _____

Objective

The purpose of this investigation is to solve a problem using scientific methodology.

Materials

Candles
Matches

Equipment

Beakers (250 mL), 2
Metric ruler
Pans for water, 2

Introduction

The **scientific method** is a way of solving problems and is used in all scientific areas. It is not a rigid procedure but rather a set of principles that is followed. It is more accurate to call it *scientific methodology* because the actual steps used for any particular problem may differ from other investigations. To understand how scientific methodology works is equivalent to understanding how scientists work.

The scientific method has a starting point but really no ending point. The first step is to recognize a problem. Then observations are made, data are organized and analyzed, and a solution is chosen. The choice of a solution starts the process again because the solution should be verified by the researcher or other people. Additionally, the initial problem may be evaluated again using different equipment. If the experiment did not verify the original hypothesis, a different hypothesis may be tested. Often, solutions to one problem suggest other questions.

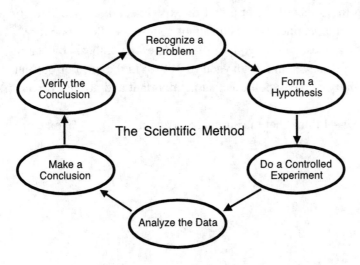

Pre-Laboratory Questions

Read the entire investigation. Answer the following questions prior to class on a separate sheet of paper. Use complete sentences if necessary.

1. What is the scientific method?

2. The scientific method is not a _?_, but rather a set of _?_.

3. Explain why scientific methodology does not have an ending point.

4. What is the first objective in scientific methodology?

Recognize a Problem

Problems in science are frequently stated as questions. A properly formed question is essential for good research. Like a road map, it provides a clear direction to go in solving a problem. A poor question, like a poor map, can result in much wasted time because of wrong turns.

In this investigation we will determine the percentage of oxygen in the air. We will start with the assumption that one of the gases in the atmosphere is oxygen, but we do not know what percentage. From this problem a scientific question can be formed.

Scientific question—What is the percentage of oxygen in the air?

Form a Hypothesis

After stating the research question, all the important information about the topic is obtained and a hypothesis is constructed. A hypothesis is a key feature in science because it formulates the scientific question in a testable form. One test of a valuable scientific idea is whether it can be proved to be true or false. This is why proposing the supposed evolutionary descent of a type of organism from the fossil record is not a part of experimental science. The hypothesized evolution of an extinct organism cannot be tested in the laboratory.

For this investigation, you will formulate a hypothesis by stating your best guess for the percentage of oxygen (0-100%) in the air. For our purposes, it is the testability of the hypothesis that is important and not its correctness.

Hypothesis—I think that the air contains about _____% oxygen.

Do a Controlled Experiment

In this section you will collect data to test your hypothesis.

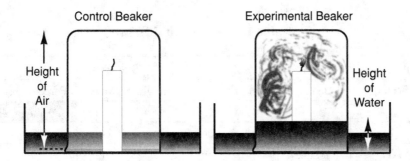

1. Measure the inside height of the beaker in centimeters.

2. Fasten two candles to the bottoms of pans with hot wax as in the diagram. The beakers must be able to cover the candles without touching the wicks.

3. Pour about 1 cm of water into the pans.

4. Place one of the beakers upside-down over one of the candles.

5. Measure the height of the water inside the beaker from the bottom of the pan. This should be less than 1 cm. Enter this measurement in Table 1, row 1/column 3. Also, subtract the height of water from the measurement you made in step 1, above, and record the difference in Table 1, rows 1-5 in column 2.

   The unlit candle is an **experimental control.** The purpose of a control is to provide a comparison. The control is just like the experimental beaker except that it lacks one item, the **experimental variable.** The experimental variable is the factor that the experiment changes to test the hypothesis. In this case, the experimental variable is the presence of the flame.

6. Light the uncovered candle.

7. Quickly place the second beaker over the burning candle.

8. Let the candle burn out, wait about twenty seconds, and then measure the height of the water inside the beaker. Subtract the height of water measurement in step 5, above, from this measurement. Write the difference in Table 1, row 2/column 3. You can assume for the purpose of this investigation that the change of the height of the water column is the same as the amount of air consumed by the candle.

9. Divide the measurement in the third column by that in the second column; then multiply by 100. This gives you the percentage of oxygen that was in the air contained in the beakers. Record this result in Table 1, row 2/column 4.

10. Carefully tip the second beaker to drain the water; then remove it and blow the smoke out of it.

11. Repeat steps 6 through 10 three more times and enter the results in Table 1 for trials 2, 3, and 4.

Analyze the Data

Placing your data in a table allows you to easily retrieve information and make calculations.

Table 1: Experimental Data

Column →	1	2	3	4
Row ↓	Beaker	Height of Air	Height of Water	Percent Oxygen
1	Control	cm	cm	
2	Trial 1	cm	cm	%
3	Trial 2	cm	cm	%
4	Trial 3	cm	cm	%
5	Trial 4	cm	cm	%
6	Average			%

Make a Conclusion

The answer, or solution, to your question is the calculated percent oxygen. However, in this investigation, there are four solutions from which to choose. Instead of selecting the "best" trial (the one that comes closest to your hypothesis), scientists usually average the trials and assume that the average is the best solution. This is a standard principle of scientific methodology since it tends to average out minor factors that are beyond the scientist's control.

To find the average percent of oxygen, add the values of the percent oxygen from trials 1 through 4 and then divide by four.

Average percent oxygen _____%   Record this value in row 6/column 4.

Verify the Conclusion

The verification process checks your procedure to see if your results can be replicated. There are two ways to verify a solution: (1) repeat the experiment and (2) compare your results with another person doing the same experiment. You have repeated your experiment three times (three replications) and now you will compare your results with other groups. Record your average for Group 1 in Table 2 and then obtain the averages from the other groups in your class. Record them in Table 2 as well. Determine the average percentage oxygen for all of the groups in your class and enter this value next to "Average" in the table.

Table 2: Averages

Group	Percent Oxygen (%)
1 (your group)	
2	
3	
4	
Average	

Discussion Questions

Write your answers in complete sentences unless otherwise indicated.

1. Define the following terms.

   a. Experimental variable _____

   _____

   b. Experimental control _____

   _____

2. Why is it important to replicate results? _____

   _____

3. What are the two ways to verify (replicate) results? _____

   _____

4. How was the height of the air and water column made objective? _____

   _____

5. What is the purpose of the hypothesis? _____

   _____

6. In the scientific method, why is it necessary to identify a problem first?

   _____

   _____

Experimental Evaluation

7. What made the water rise in the beaker with the burning candle? _____

   _____

8. What gas did you assume was burned in the beaker? _____

   _____

9. How did your hypothesis compare with your data? _____

   _____

10. How was your final solution (the percentage of oxygen) chosen? _____

    _____

11. Do you think this method will always give the best answer? Explain. _____

    _____

    _____

12. Why is it not possible to obtain an exact answer? _____

    _____

13. Why didn't all of your trials come out the same? _____

    _____

    _____

14 Why didn't the other groups' averages come out the same? _____

    _____

15. What observations produced data in this investigation? _____

_____

16. What is the purpose of a control? _____

_____

17. In this experiment, what was the difference between the control and the experimental beaker? _____

18. (Optional) What inferences and assumptions were made from these observations? _____

_____

_____

_____

_____

_____

2B INVESTIGATION
Scientific Reports

Objective

The purpose of this investigation is to introduce the proper form for scientific reports and to illustrate how the scientific method supports this form.

Materials List

Bleach solution
Distilled water
Sugar
Table salt

Equipment List

Alligator clips, 2
Battery (6 V, with binding posts)
Beakers (250 mL), 2
Graduated cylinder (100 mL)
Insulated copper wire
Metal strips (at least 15 cm long), 2
Miniature lamp base
Miniature light bulb
Teaspoon

Introduction

After scientists perform experiments, they publish their work so that other scientists will know what they have done and can verify the results. There are usually four sections in these reports that incorporate the steps of the scientific method: **Introduction, Materials and Procedures, Results,** and **Discussion.** The Introduction states the problem to be tested and gives any related information. The Materials and Procedures section states the equipment to be used, gives the steps to follow, and provides diagrams. The observations are recorded and the data are organized in the Results section. At this point, the investigator often verifies the work by repeating the experiment several times. In the Discussion the investigator states the reasons for the choice of solutions, gives other problems suggested by the research, and further verifies the work by reporting similar experiments performed by other scientists.

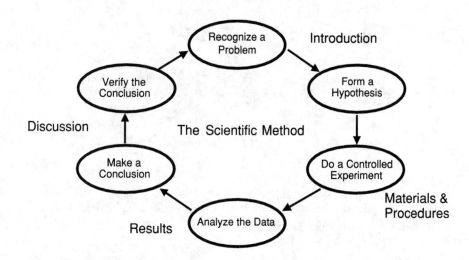

Background

You have probably been told that water does not conduct electricity, yet you have also been told to get out of a swimming pool during a lightning storm. This seems to be a contradiction! An appropriate question for the lifeguard while you are standing on the side of the pool is "Why should I get out of the pool since water does not conduct electricity?" In this investigation you will answer that question. You will use a light bulb to detect electrical current. When the light bulb is not lit, there is no significant current flowing through the water. However, when the bulb is lit, it is as if lightning hit the swimming pool and you "light" up.

Pre-Laboratory Questions

Read the entire investigation. Answer the following questions prior to class on a separate sheet of paper. Use complete sentences.

1. Give the purpose of each of the following parts of a report.

   a. Introduction—

   b. Materials and Procedures—

   c. Results—

   d. Discussion—

2. State your research question.

3. State your hypothesis.

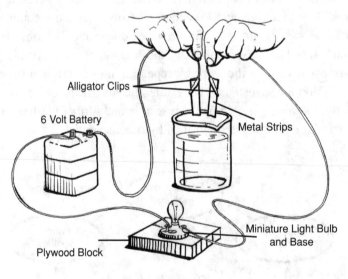

Figure 1

Procedure

1. Pour 150 mL of distilled water into a *clean* 250 mL beaker. Label this beaker **1** with an erasable marker.

2. Place 150 mL of the mixture of bleach and distilled water into a second 250 mL beaker. Label this beaker **2**.

3. Assemble the circuit-testing apparatus according to Figure 1.

4. Touch the metal pieces together to see if the light works. By touching the metal pieces, you create a closed electrical circuit.

   A **closed circuit** means that there is a continuous electrical path, allowing the electricity to make a complete circuit and thus light the light bulb. An **open circuit** means that the electricity cannot follow a complete path because there is an interruption in the path.

5. Place the two metal strips in beaker **1** to determine if the distilled water conducts electricity. Do not let the pieces of metal touch each other in the water. Avoid touching the metal with your fingers. Record your results in the data table under Trial 1 for distilled water.

6. Place the two metal pieces in beaker **2** and observe the light bulb. Record your results in data table.

7. Pour the contents of the beakers down the sink and rinse beaker **2** *thoroughly* in tap water. Rinse the metal strips in tap water.

8. Mix 1 teaspoon of salt and 150 mL distilled water in beaker **1**. Mix 1 teaspoon of sugar and 150 mL distilled water in beaker **2**. Determine the conductivity of each of these solutions using the same procedure as above. Rinse the electrodes between each test. Record your results in the appropriate spaces in the data table under Trial 1.

9. Repeat the experiment if possible and record the results under Trial 2.

10. Record the results from two other groups in the data table under groups 2 and 3.

Results

Data Table: Conductivity of Solutions

Solution	Conductive? (Yes or No)			
	Trial 1	Trial 2	Group 2	Group 3
Distilled water				
Water and bleach				
Water and salt				
Water and sugar				

Discussion Questions

Answer the following questions in complete sentences.

1. What information does the background to this investigation give about the conductivity of water? _____

   _____

2. What causes water to conduct electricity? _____

   _____

3. What kind of compound in swimming pools causes the water to conduct?

_____

_____

4. What are open and closed circuits? _____

_____

_____

_____

Experimental Evaluation

5. State two ways that this experiment was replicated. _____

_____

_____

6. Which solution was the control? _____

_____

7. What is the purpose of the control? _____

_____

8. What is an experimental variable? _____

_____

9. What was the experimental variable in this experiment? _____

_____

10. Why was it necessary to touch the metal electrodes together prior to placing them into the solutions? _____

_____

11. Is the phrase "one teaspoon" objective or subjective? Explain. _____

_____

_____

_____

12. Did all of the three mixtures conduct electricity? If not, which did not? If not all water solutions conduct electricity, how would you have to modify your hypothesis? _____

_____

_____

13. (Optional) The light bulb did not light up when testing the distilled water. Does that prove that distilled water does not conduct any electricity? Explain.

_____

_____

Preparing a Scientific Report

Write a brief scientific report using the information discussed in this investigation. Your teacher will give you the specific guidelines for report length and format. The content should be organized in the following sections: Introduction, Materials and Procedures, Results, and Discussion. You should try to express the problem in your own words, make your own diagrams and tables, and describe the procedure and the results after thinking about the reasons in complete thoughts.

3A APPLICATIONS
Significant Digits/Reading Scales

Objectives

The purpose of this exercise is to

1. Introduce the concept of uncertainty in all measurements.

2, Introduce the use of significant digits and their use in scientific activities.

3. Correctly report the measurements made with common laboratory equipment.

Introduction

Counting

Objects that are counted are reported as exact numbers. When numbering a group of people, for instance, you wouldn't say that there are 12.5 people in the room. A whole number is the only correct way to report such a count. Counting any group of objects is handled the same way. If your teacher gave you a box of paper clips, you could report to him exactly how many paper clips are in that box.

Uncertainty in Measurements

What if you were asked to measure the length of one of the paper clips? This would also appear to be rather simple. If you used a ruler that was calibrated only in centimeters, it would appear to fall somewhere between 3 and 4 centimeters. What would you report? You would probably report an estimate of how far past the 3 cm mark you thought it went, perhaps 3.1 cm.

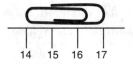

Now, however, your teacher gives you a ruler that is calibrated not only to centimeters but also to millimeters. "Aha," you say. "Now I can give my teacher an exact measurement!" You carefully measure the paperclip and see that the end of the paper clip falls somewhere between 3.1 cm and 3.2 cm. Perhaps with this new ruler you could tell your teacher that the paper clip is 3.13 cm long.

Because you had a measuring device that had greater resolution (i.e., smaller graduations or divisions), you could report the measurement with greater precision. However, because it is not marked with even smaller divisions, you again have had to make an estimate of where between those two measurements the end of the paper clip falls. This example illustrates the uncertainty in making *any* kind of measurement. No matter how small the graduations of your measuring device, you will still have to estimate the last digit that you report. It is for this reason that it is impossible to state that a measurement is exact.

Precision and Accuracy

When you can make a measurement using an instrument with a greater number of subdivisions in its scale, the measurement will be more consistently reproduced. In the above example, having ten classmates measure the same paperclip with a millimeter scale will produce ten readings close to 3.1 cm while having the same group make the measurement with a centimeter scale could produce a variety of readings from 3.0 cm to 3.2 cm. *The ability to reproduce a measurement consistently is one definition of* **precision.** The more graduations per unit of measurement an instrument has, the more precise it is. Another term that is often used instead of precision is **accuracy.** *Accuracy refers to how close the instrument can measure to the actual measurement.* Wooden meter sticks can expand and shrink with humidity and metal ruler change length with temperature. Balances get dropped and parts wear. Graduated cylinders are mass-produced and their volumes are not exactly the same. These instruments' accuracies are determined by comparing them against instrument *standards* that are maintained by governments around the world. As you can see, precision and accuracy are two different concepts. For measurements in the laboratory in this course, we will be mainly concerned about the precision of our measurements.

Significant Digits

In any *measurement,* all the digits that are known to be certain (the digits that can be determined from marks on the measuring tool) are reported, plus one that is estimated. This combination of digits is called the **significant digits** of the measurement. When you see a written measurement, you should be able to tell how finely the scale of the measuring device was subdivided (its precision). For instance, a measurement reported as 24.5 g tells you that the balance was only calibrated (marked) with divisions of 1 g and that the last decimal number was estimated. A number reported as 24.506 g indicates that a more sensitive balance was used, one that was calibrated to the nearest 0.01 g and, again, that the last decimal number was estimated. A scientific measurement should never be written with greater or fewer than the permissible number of significant digits. It is important for you to learn how to correctly report the measurements you will be making in future investigations.

Rules

To help you make and report correct scientific measurements, the following list of rules should be followed:

1. All measurements with metric instruments should be reported as decimal numbers, not fractions (0.5 rather than $\frac{1}{2}$).

2. All measurements *must include units* when reported. To report a length of 6.02 is meaningless unless the units used for the measurement are also reported.

3. Measurements must include all digits that are *certain* (based on the markings on the measuring instrument).

4. Measurements must include ONE *estimated digit* to the nearest tenth ($\frac{1}{10}$) of the smallest *decimal* (multiple of 10) calibration marked. This is often called the **least significant digit** of the measurement.

Example: If a balance's smallest calibration marks are 0.1 g, the estimated digit of any measurement will be to the nearest 0.01 g.

Example: If a graduated cylinder's smallest calibration is $\frac{1}{2}$ mL, the estimated digit of any measurement will be to the nearest 0.1 mL (the smallest <u>decimal</u> calibration is 1 mL; $\frac{1}{2}$ is NOT a decimal calibration).

Example: When measuring the length of an object with a ruler calibrated to millimeters, the reading appears to fall exactly on the line 3.4 cm. You would report the measurement as 3.40 cm. Since you are able to estimate to 0.01 cm ($\frac{1}{10}$ mm) with this ruler (see Rules 3 & 4), you must include the final zero to indicate the precision of your measuring device.

Note: When the calibrations are very close together, visually estimating to one-tenth of the interval is impractical. In these cases, estimating to the nearest 0.5 ($\frac{1}{2}$) of the interval is acceptable.

Interpreting Measurements

For each of the following measurements, state the digit that has been estimated and give the smallest calibration of the instrument used to make the measurement.

	Estimated Digit	**Calibration**
Example: 37.7 mL	7	1 mL
1. 15.02 g	_____	_____
2. 7.43 cm	_____	_____
3. −2.9°C	_____	_____

Reading Rulers

On the ruler below, the smallest calibration (marked interval) is 0.1 cm (1 mm). The measurement can be estimated to the nearest 0.01 cm (0.1 mm). Write the measurements for the following points on the ruler. The first two have been done as examples.

A. 8.13 cm

B. 8.50 cm

C. _____

D. _____

E. _____

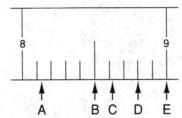

Reading Balances

Below is a portion of the scale of a mass balance that measures in grams. The smallest calibration is _____ g. Therefore, the measurement can be estimated to one-tenth of the interval, which is _____ g. Report the measurements at the following points, including the correct units.

A. _____

B. _____

C. _____

D. _____

E. _____

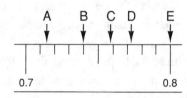

On a less precise balance below, the smallest decimal calibration is _____ g. The measurement can be estimated to one-tenth of the interval, which is _____ g. Report the measurements at the following points including the correct units.

A. _____

B. _____

C. _____

D. _____

E. _____

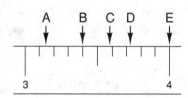

Reading Graduated Cylinders

Measurements made with graduated cylinders follow the same rules as for rulers. The last digit is an estimate of one-tenth of the interval. The smallest marked decimal calibrations on the cylinder below are _____ mL. Therefore, the measurement can be estimated to the nearest _____ mL. Because of the effects of surface tension, the top of the liquid in a cylinder will form a curve called a *meniscus*. The measurement should always be read at the bottom of the meniscus with the eye level with it. Report the measurements at the following points including the correct units.

A. _____

B. _____

C. _____

D. _____

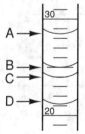

The graduated cylinder below is a small cylinder and is calibrated differently. The smallest decimal calibration is _____ mL. (Note that there are only five 1/5 mL marks, so these are not *decimal* calibrations.) The measurement can, therefore, be estimated to the nearest _____ mL (see example 2 under Rule 4 above). Report the measurements at the following points including the correct units.

A. _____

B. _____

C. _____

D. _____

Reading Thermometers

The thermometer below is calibrated to _____ °C. The measurement can be estimated to the nearest _____ °C. Report the measurements at the following points including the correct units.

A. _____

B. _____

C. _____

D. _____

Reading Beakers

Beakers are not made for volumetric measurements. For example, the beaker below can only approximate measurements up to 80 mL. Answer the following questions for the purpose of practice only. The beaker's smallest decimal calibration is _____ mL. The measurement can be estimated to the nearest _____ mL. Report the measurements at the following points including the correct units.

A. _____

B. _____

C. _____

D. _____

3B APPLICATIONS
Significant Digits in Calculations

Name _____

Date _____ Hour _____

Objectives

The purpose of these exercises is to

1. Learn how to identify the number of significant digits in a measurement.

2. Review how to round numbers correctly.

3. Learn the rules for calculations involving significant digits.

Introduction

You learned in Applications 3A that scientists indicate the precision of their measurements by using significant digits (SDs). Recall that *precision* refers to the repeatability of a measurement, which is related to how finely divided the scale of the instrument is. *Accuracy* refers to how close a measurement is to the actual value, which is associated with quality of construction of the instrument and its calibration against a known standard. Scientists regularly have to make calculations using the measurements they have taken in the laboratory. In order to report their results in a way that correctly shows the precision of their measurements, they have developed rules for rounding the results of these calculations. Before you learn these rules, however, you need to know how to determine the number of significant digits in a measurement and review the rules for rounding off numbers.

Determining the Number of Significant Digits

Before we discuss how to perform calculations using measurements, we must first determine the number of SDs in each measurement using the following rules:

1. Significant digits apply *only to measurements*. They do not apply to . . .

   a. Exact numbers obtained from counting (twice, dozen, six students, etc.)

   b. Pure numbers (any real number that is not a measurement: 29, $\frac{1}{2}$, $\sqrt{2}$, etc.)

   c. Definitions (60 seconds per minute, 100 cm per meter, etc.)

2. All non-zero digits are significant. (375.42 cm has 5 SDs)

3. Dealing with zeros

   a. All zeros *between* non-zero digits are significant. (ex.: 208.5 m has 4 SDs)

   b. All zeros in a measurement having a decimal point are significant, except for *leading zeros* (see Figure 1a).

   > example: 65.10 g has 4 SDs
   > example: 0.0651 g has 3 SDs

c. *Trailing zeros* in a measurement *without a decimal point* (see Figure 1b) are *not* significant. If the measurement *has* a decimal point, then all trailing zeros are significant (Figure 1a).

example: 5300 cm has 2 SDs

example: 530.0 cm has 4 SDs

a. 0.050 cm   **b.2,050 mm**

Leading Zeroes   Trailing Zero   Trailing Zero

Figure 1

d. To indicate precision of a measurement with significant trailing zeros, use scientific notation. ALL DIGITS IN THE DECIMAL PORTION OF SCIENTIFIC NOTATION ARE SIGNIFICANT.

> *Example:* 380,000 m that was measured to the nearest 1000 meters should be written 3.80×10^5 m. If it was measured to the nearest 100 meters, it should be written 3.800×10^5 m.

Because not all zeros are significant, the number of significant digits is not always the same as the number of digits. Study the following chart to help you learn the rules and complete the exercises below.

Examples

	Measurement	Number of Digits	Number of Significant Digits	Rule
1.	213 m	3	3	2
2.	210 cm	3	2	3c
3.	3.01 g	3	3	3a
4.	5.200 L	4	4	3b, c
5.	0.031 km	4	2	3b
6.	1.7×10^4 mm	2*	2	3d

Adding a zero before the decimal in example 5 is a standard practice to improve clarity.

*In scientific notation, only the digits in the decimal portion are counted.

Practice Counting Significant Digits

State the correct number of SDs or write NA if SDs are not applicable. In the equations, look at the underlined portion.

a. 123 cm _____

b. 0.012 cm _____

c. 2100 cm _____

d. 1 gross _____

e. 0.0101 cm _____

f. 1 km/h $\doteq$ <u>0.621 mi./h</u> _____

g. 2.01 cm _____

h. 0.0102 cm _____

i. 1020. cm _____

j. 1.020 cm _____

k. 2,020 _____

l. 1 gal. $\doteq$ <u>3.786 L</u> _____

m. 2001 cm _____   p. 0.0010 cm _____

n. 2000 cm _____   q. 5.0 cm _____

o. 1.03 cm _____   r. 1 min. = 60 s _____

Rounding Numbers

Answers obtained using calculators often have many more decimal places than necessary or permissible. To arrive at the correct answer from calculations involving measurements, we need to round the answer to the correct numerical place. We will use the following familiar rounding rules for our work in this course:

1. Determine the required numerical place to round to in the measurement.

2. If the first digit to the right of the required place is 4 or less, drop it and all remaining digits to the right.

   Note: If the required place is to the left of the (assumed) position of the decimal point, fill in the empty places to the left of the decimal point with zeros.

3. If the first digit to the right of the required place is 5 or greater, add one to the required place, drop all remaining digits to the right, and replace with zeros, if required, as in Rule 2 above.

4. Decimal points should not be added after trailing zeros unless the ones place is significant.

   Examples:

   a. Round 38,462 m to the hundreds place   38,500 m

   b. Round 38,462 m to the thousands place   38,000 m

   c. Round 0.561 m to the tenths place   0.6 m

Practice Rounding Measurements

Round the following measurements to the hundredths place:

a. 10.0944 m _____   d. 1.0149 L _____

b. 0.1234 s _____   e. 1.0846 km _____

c. 0.0999 km _____   f. 23.095 MHz _____

Round the following measurements to the tens place:

a. 123 cm _____   d. 89 s _____

b. 2354 mm _____   e. 544.9 mL _____

c. 294.1 m _____   f. 765.23 m/s _____

Rules for Calculations Using Significant Digits

Rules for calculations have been developed to ensure that results reported correctly show the precision of the measurements made in the laboratory. Let's say that you measured the edge of one side of a rectangle to be 2.38 cm and the other to be 5.79 cm using a metric ruler marked in millimeters (0.1 cm). What area would you report for this rectangle? The calculator answer for this product is 2.38 cm $\times$ 5.79 cm = 13.7802 cm². Let us analyze this answer. In the expanded multiplication problem shown, all circled digits are either estimated or result from operations performed with estimated digits.

$$
\begin{array}{r}
5.7\text{⑨ cm} \\
\times\ 2.3\text{⑧ cm} \\
\hline
\text{④⑥③②} \\
1\ 73\text{⑦} \\
11\ 5\text{⑧} \\
\hline
13.\text{⑦}8\ \text{⑥②}\ \text{cm}^2
\end{array}
$$

The results of calculations must follow the same rules as the original measurements—they may have only one estimated digit. Allowing more than this would indicate your original measurements were more precise than they actually were. This would not be honest reporting. All workers, and Christians in particular, must be honest when reporting their results. In this example, the answer must be rounded to the tenths place, 13.8 cm². It is important to know how many significant digits to use when reporting your results. Study the following rules and answer the problems below.

Basic Rules for Operations with Significant Digits

1. *Multiplication and Division*—Answers to problems resulting from **multiplying** or **dividing** two or more measurements can have no more significant figures than the factor, divisor, or dividend with the fewest SDs. Round the result to correct.

   Example: 2 cm $\times$ 4.55 cm = 9.10 cm²

   Since only one SD is allowed, the answer $\approx$ 9 cm².

2. *Addition and Subtraction*—Answers to problems resulting from **addition** or **subtraction** of two or more measurements can be no more precise than the least precise addend, minuend, or subtrahend.

   Example: 30 g + 22.5 g = 52.5 g

   The least precise measurement or the highest-placed estimated digit in any addend is the tens place in 30 g. Therefore, the answer $\approx$ 50 g.

Advanced Rules for Operations with Significant Digits (Optional)

3. The **multiplication** or **division** of a measurement by a *pure* number should not produce a result that is less precise or more precise than the original measurement. Round the result to a number having the same precision as the original measurement (that is, the least significant digit is in the same place as the original measurement).

   Example:

   Compute the radius of a circle given that the diameter is 1.35 cm. $d = \dfrac{r}{2}$, therefore, $r = 1.35$ cm $\div\ 2 = 0.675$ cm.

   Due to the precision of the original measurement, you must round the result to 0.68 cm.

Example:

Compute the surface area of a cube if one face (B) is 2.25 cm². *A = 6B,* therefore 6 × 2.25 cm² = 13.5 cm². Because the original face area was precise to hundredths of a cm², the final result must reflect this precision: *A* = 13.50 cm².

Recall that multiplying by a pure number is just repetitive addition, so the basic addition rules apply.

4. In any given problem, all similar, simultaneous operations that must be performed should be calculated in one step before rounding to proper SDs. Rounding after each step of a multiple-step problem introduces unnecessary errors.

   Example: Find the volume of a rectangular solid 4 cm × 1.10 cm × 2.1 cm. The product by calculator is 9.24 cm³. This product is allowed one SD (Rule 1), so the result is rounded to $V \approx 9$ cm³.

   But if you find 4 cm × 1.10 cm = 4.40 cm², this is rounded to 4 cm² (1 SD). If you then multiply 4 cm² by 2.1 cm, the answer is 8.4 cm³. When you round this result to one SD your final answer is <u>8 cm³</u>. Compared to 9 cm³, this has an 11% error!

5. When performing a connected series of multiplication/division and addition/subtraction operations, be sure to apply the appropriate SD rules to the applicable steps before going on to a different type of operation. In other words, do not apply multiplication/division rules to the results of addition/subtraction, and vice versa.

Practice Calculating with Significant Digits

Report the results of the following calculations in raw form and using the appropriate number of SDs. Give the operations rule number that applies to the calculation.

	Raw Answer	Rounded Answer	Rule Number
1. 6.3 cm × 8.05 cm			
2. 40.2 mL + 27 mL			
3. 6 mL − 2.5 mL			
4. 17.0 mm × 5.4 mm			
5. 19.80 g − 7.3 g			
6. (See word problem below)			
7. (See word problem below)			
8. 16.5 mm ÷ 2			
9. 5.5 mL × 3			
10. 7.2 cm × 5 cm × 1.25 cm			
11. (See word problem below)			
12. (See word problem below)			

Word Problems (Show your work.)

6. Mr. Rodriguez, the science teacher, needs to determine the volume of a block of wood. Its dimensions are length—2.5 cm, width—2.00 cm, height—1.0 cm. What is the volume of the cube? _____

_____

7. Dr. Dickson added 63.7 mL of water to 58.4 mL of sodium hydroxide solution. What is the volume of the new solution? _____

_____

11. The route that Shane jogs every day is 10.9 km long. Shane's little brother wants to run a distance one-fourth as long. What distance will Shane have to measure for his brother? _____

_____

12. A missionary is going to carpet three classrooms in his school. The rooms measure 3.3 m × 3.95 m, 5.4 m × 6 m, and 7.35 m × 8.08 m. What is the total area of carpet he must buy? _____

_____

_____

_____

_____

Name _____

Date _____ Hour _____

Objectives

The purposes of this investigation are to

1. Become familiar with the use of basic laboratory instruments.

2. Verify that exact measurements are not possible.

Equipment

Mass balance
Metal specific gravity cylinder or other solid object
Metric ruler (1 per student)
Thermometers (Celsius/Fahrenheit scales), 4

Introduction

Scientists use many different instruments to aid their senses. These instruments help make their observations more objective. For example, instead of saying that the water is hot (subjective), a person can measure the temperature of the water with a thermometer and say it is 110 °F (objective). This appears to settle the question of the water temperature, but does it really? Did that person mean that the temperature is exactly 110 °F or approximately 110 °F? Can a person assert that the temperature is exactly 110 °F? In this investigation, we are going to answer the question "Is it possible to make exact measurements?"

Pre-Laboratory Questions

Read the entire investigation. Answer the following questions prior to class on a separate sheet of paper. Use complete sentences.

1. What do scientists use to aid their senses in making observations?

2. What is an objective observation?

3. What is a subjective observation?

4. Which is more desirable when making scientific observations, objectivity or subjectivity? Explain.

5. State your research question.

6. State your hypothesis.

Procedure

You will be performing a series of measurements using three different common laboratory instruments. In addition to gaining practice obtaining accurate measurements, you will practice recording data using the correct number of significant digits. Review the rules for recording measurements in Applications 3A and 3B, if necessary.

A. Balances

1. Measure the mass of the cylinder or another object. Do not reveal this measurement to your team members until they have made their measurements. Record your measurement in Table 1.

2. Return all of the balance sliders to the zero position.

3. After the other people on your team have measured the same object, record their results in Table 1.

4. Average the values for the mass of the object (add the values and divide by the number of readings).

B. Rulers

1. Draw a line on the side of this page 10 inches long. Try to make your line exactly 10 inches.

2. Measure the line in centimeters as precisely as possible, using the measurement rules you have learned.

   10 inches = _____ cm

   Calculate the length of one inch in centimeters.

   1 inch = _____ cm

Parallax Error

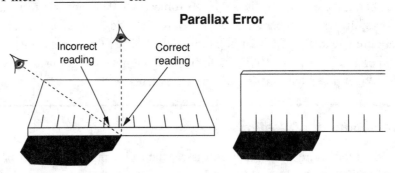

Parallax error occurs when the scale on the ruler and your line of sight to the object being measured are not correctly aligned. When placing the ruler flat on the page, the scale you are reading should be placed directly in front of you so that your line of sight is perpendicular to the edge of the ruler at the point of measurement. If the scale is placed to the right of your eye, the reading will appear to be farther to the left on the scale than the correct reading. This error can also be avoided by placing the ruler on its edge so that the scale directly contacts the line or object being measured. Parallax error is one of the most common measurement errors experienced in the laboratory. Always be alert for it.

3. Draw a line on your paper 11.20 cm long.

4. Place the ruler flat on the paper. Read the measurement of the line you drew in step 3 perpendicular to the ruler. Without moving the ruler, alter your line of sight to the scale so that you are reading it from far to the left. Observe how the apparent measurement differs as you alter your line of sight. Record your measurement from this position. _____ How does this compare with the original length? _____

_____

5. Place the ruler on edge as in the diagram on the right, above. Again, as you measure the line, alter your line of sight to the scale. It should not affect the reading. This is a more reliable way to measure something.

6. Measure the length and width of your lab manual to hundredths of a centimeter and record the measurements in Table 2.

7. After the other people on your team have measured the same manual, obtain their measurements and write them in Table 2.

8. Average the measurements of the lab manual in Table 2.

C. Thermometers

1. Measure the room temperature in °C with four thermometers and record this value in Table 3. (Be sure to use the correct significant digits as discussed in Applications 3A and 3B.)

2. Obtain four room temperature readings from each of two other teams and write these in Table 3.

3. Average the values from each team and determine the average of the averages (grand mean).

4. (Optional) Measure room temperature in °F. _____ °F

Results

Table 1: Object Mass

Team Member	Mass (g)
Average	

Table 2: Book Measurements

Team Member	Length (cm)	Width (cm)
Average		

Table 3: Room Temperature

Thermometer	Yours (°C)	Other #1 (°C)	Other #2 (°C)
#1			
#2			
#3			
#4			
Average			
Grand Mean			

Discussion Questions

Write your answers in complete sentences. Try to explain your answers.

1. Were all the object and book measurements the same? If not, give some reasons. _____

   _____

2. When you measured the room temperature with different thermometers, were all the values the same? If not, what are some sources of error? ____

   _____

   _____

3. In Table 3, how far apart are the averages of the three sets of readings compared to the spread of the individual measurements? _____

   _____

4. Why is it sometimes necessary to measure something more than once and then take an average? _____

   _____

5. When a person says that the temperature is 110 °F, is this an exact value or an approximation? Explain. _____

   _____

   _____

6. Explain parallax error. _____

   _____

Experimental Evaluation

7. Did this investigation answer the research question? Explain. _____

   _____

   _____

8. Give two ways that the measurement of room temperature was replicated.

   a. _____

   _____

   b. _____

9. (Optional) Having established the difficulty of obtaining exact measurements, give two other research questions suggested by this investigation. _____

   _____

   _____

   _____

3D INVESTIGATION

Density

Objectives

The purpose of this investigation is to

1. Gain experience in the use of laboratory equipment.

2. Calculate the density of several objects.

3. Apply the principles of significant digits to calculations.

Materials

Rectangular wooden block
Sewing thread

Equipment

Beaker (250 mL)
Eyedropper
Graduated cylinder (100 mL)
Mass balance
Metal specific gravity cylinder or other
    metal object
Metric ruler
Overflow can

Introduction

If you had a chance to play with a professional football team, the members of that team would probably consider you a fairly light player. Suppose that after the football game, if you were still alive, you looked after your neighbor's six-year-old darling. The six-year-old would think you were a big, heavy person. The terms *heavy* and *light* are subjective terms that represent personal opinions. The ideas of heaviness and lightness are scientifically useful, but they must be described objectively. For example, a block of lead is heavy for its size and will, consequently, sink in water. However, the same size block of cork is light and will float. To make the relative heaviness of an object quantifiable, we use the concept of **density.** The density of an object or substance is the amount of mass in each unit of its volume. Since mass and volume are measurable, objectivity is gained.

Pre-Laboratory Questions

Read the entire investigation. Answer the following questions prior to class on a separate sheet of paper. Use complete sentences if necessary.

1. Which two properties of an object do you have to measure to calculate the density of an object?

2. Describe the two different ways volume will be determined in this investigation.

3. What is the accepted density for water?

4. Give the formula for the volume of

   a. a cylinder.

   b. a rectangular block.

5. How do you find the percent difference between two numbers?

Procedures

A. *The Density of Water*

1. Volume

a. Measure 50.0 mL of water into your graduated cylinder. (Note that this measurement must be precise to one-tenth of a milliliter.) You may find that using an eyedropper is helpful to make any final adjustments in level.

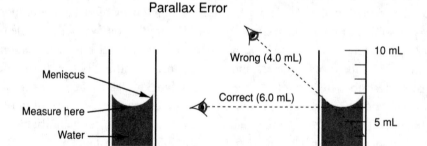

Parallax Error

To avoid parallax error in reading a graduated cylinder, you must place your eye so that it is level with the bottom of the meniscus. If you read the level at an angle (either from above or below), your recorded value will not be correct. The above diagram illustrates this problem.

b. Record 50.0 mL in the data table on page 50 in the "Volume" column and set the water-filled graduated cylinder aside.

2. *Mass*

a. Find the mass of a dry beaker using a balance. Record this value in ❶ below. Why is it important that the beaker be dry? _____

_____

_____

b. Carefully pour the 50.0 mL of water from the graduated cylinder into the beaker. How would spilling some water or leaving water in the cylinder affect the results? _____

_____

_____

c. Find the mass of the beaker and water together. Record this value in ❷.

d. Subtract ❶ from ❷ and record this value in ❸. This is the mass of the water. Record this value in the data table in the "Mass" column.

    ❷ Mass of water and beaker   _____ g

    ❶ Mass of beaker   − _____ g

    ❸ Mass of water   = _____ g

3. Density

Density is the ratio of the mass of a substance to its volume. It is obtained by dividing the mass by the volume.

a. Divide the water's mass by its volume to calculate the density. Record this value in the data table under the "Density" column. Include the proper units (g/mL).

b. The density of pure water is 1.00 g/mL. If the density is not within the range 0.95 g/mL − 1.05 g/mL, repeat the steps above.

B. *The Density of a Metal Cylinder*

1. Volume by Water Displacement

a. Measure 50.0 mL of water into the graduated cylinder. Record this value in ❶ below.

b. Tie a piece of thread to the metal cylinder and carefully lower it into the water in the graduated cylinder. **Caution:** Do not drop the metal object into the cylinder. Doing so can break glass cylinders.

c. Measure the combined volume of the water and metal cylinder. Record this value in ❷ below.

d. Subtract ❶ from ❷ and record this value in ❸. If you cannot perform step 2 because your metal object is not a cylinder, record the value from ❸ in the data table under the "Volume" column and skip to step 3.

    ❷ Volume of water and metal   _____ mL

    ❶ Volume of water   − _____ mL

    ❸ Volume of metal (V_D)   = _____ mL

2. Volume by Measurement

If you are using standard cylindrical metal specific gravity samples, you can calculate their volume from their dimensions.

a. Measure the cylinder's diameter (d) to one-hundredth of a centimeter. $d = $ _____ cm

b. Measure the cylinder's length (geometrically equal to its height [h]) to the same precision. $h = $ _____ cm

c. The formula for the volume of a cylinder is $V = \pi r^2 h$. You must find the radius (r) of the cylinder before you can use this formula.

d. Calculate the radius: $r = \dfrac{d}{2} = \dfrac{cm}{2} = $ _____ cm. Recall from Applications 3B that this result cannot have greater precision than your original measurement.

e. Compute the volume of the cylinder from measurements: $V_M = $ _____ cm³. If you are not observing SDs, round to hundredths of a cubic centimeter. Record this value in the "Volume" column in the data table.

f. Calculate the percent difference in the volumes found by displacement and by calculation. Divide the difference in the volumes by the average of the two volumes (v_{avg}). Multiply this result by 100%.

$$\text{Percent difference} = \frac{|V_M - V_D|}{V_{avg}} \times 100\% = \underline{} \%$$

If the difference is greater than 5%, review your calculations in step 2f. If these are accurate, repeat steps 1 and 2 in this section.

3. Mass

Measure the mass of the dry metal cylinder using a balance and record this value in the data table under the "Mass" column.

4. Density

Calculate the density of the cylinder by dividing the mass by the volume recorded in the data table. Record this value in the data table under the "Density" column.

C. The Density of Wood (Optional)

1. Volume by Measurement

a. Measure the length, width, and height of a wooden block in cm. (Estimate dimensions to hundredths of a cm.)

Length _____ Width _____ Height _____

b. Calculate the volume of the block by multiplying the three measurements. If you are observing proper significant digits, how many are allowed? _____ cm

If you are not observing significant digits, round the volume to two decimal places.

c. Record the resulting value in the data table under the "Volume" column.

2. Volume by Water Displacement

a. Measure the mass of the wooden block according to step 3 below *before* determining the volume by water displacement. Why is this necessary?

_____

b. Fill the overflow can with water. Overfill it slightly so that some water pours out the spout.

c. When the water has stopped dripping from the spout, place a dry graduated cylinder under the spout of the can.

d. Float the wooden block in the can. Using three fingers to steady the block, slowly push it under the water until its upper face is just level with the water's surface. Be careful that your fingertips do not go under water. You do not want to include the volume of your fingers in the measurement. Once it has been fully submerged, wait until the water stops dripping out of the spout. Remove the graduated cylinder before releasing the block.

e. The volume of the water that has spilled into the graduated cylinder is the volume of the wooden block.

Volume by water displacement: $V_D =$ _____

Volume by calculation of measurements: $V_M =$ _____

f. Calculate the percent difference in the volumes. Divide the difference in the volumes by the average of V_M and V_D. Multiply this by 100%.

$$\text{Percent difference} = \frac{|V_M - V_D|}{V_{avg.}} \times 100\% = \underline{\hspace{1cm}}\%$$

If the difference is greater than 5%, review your calculations in step 2f. If these are accurate, repeat steps 1 and 2 in this section.

3. Mass

Find the mass of the wooden block and record this value in the data table under the "Mass" column.

4. Density

a. Calculate the density of the wooden block and record this value in the data table under the "Density" column.

b. If the value is greater than 1.00 g/mL, you need to repeat the measurements for the mass and the density of the wooden block. Why?

_____

_____

Results

Data Table: Densities

Object	Mass (g)	Volume (mL)	Density (g/mL)
Water			
Metal			
Wood			

Discussion Questions

1. The density of a substance is the ratio of its _____ and its _____.

2. What is the unit for density? _____

3. The density indicates the number of grams in one mL of a substance. Complete the following statements.

   a. A density of 3.0 g/mL means that there are 3.0 grams in 1 mL.

   b. A density of 5.1 g/mL means that there are _____ in _____.

   c. A density of 0.9 g/mL means that there are _____ in _____.

4. Which substance in question 3 (a, b, or c) is the least dense? Explain the reason for your choice. _____
   _____

5. Assume that the density of water is 1 g/mL. 30 mL of water will have a mass of _____.

6. Since the ratio of cubic centimeters (cm³) to milliliters is 1, 40 cm³ is another way of saying _____ mL.

7. A piece of metal has a mass of 120 g and a volume of 30 mL. What is its density? _____

8. A piece of wood has a volume of 200 mL and a mass of 100 g. What is its density? _____

Experimental Evaluation

9. Which of the materials in this investigation is the most dense? Why? _____
   _____

10. What appears to be the relationship between density and the ability to float in water? _____
    _____

11. Describe the method of finding the volume of an object by water displacement in a graduated cylinder. _____
    _____
    _____
    _____

12. (Optional) Of the two methods you used to find the volume of the metal cylinder, which do you think is the more precise? _____

_____

_____

13. (Optional) When would it be preferable to find the volume of an object by water displacement rather than by measuring its dimensions? Give an example. _____

_____

_____

_____

14. (Optional) What are some difficulties with using the overflow displacement method to find the volume of small objects? _____

_____

_____

_____

4A INVESTIGATION
Chemical and Physical Changes

Objectives

The purpose of this investigation is to

1. Learn the difference between chemical and physical changes.

2. Learn the difference between evidence and proof that a chemical change has occurred.

Materials

Aluminum foil
Ammonia
Baking soda
Epsom salts
Sugar
Table salt
Vinegar

Equipment

Beaker (250 mL)
Beakers (100 mL), 2
Bunsen burner
Bunsen burner lighter
Graduated cylinder (100 mL)
Large rubber band
Teaspoon
Tripod
Wire gauze

Introduction

Chemistry is primarily the study of chemical and physical changes of matter, while physics focuses on physical processes involving matter. A **physical change** occurs when a substance simply changes shape, form, or state (gas, liquid, or solid)—its identity is not altered. Examples of physical changes include boiling, evaporation, melting, bending, tearing, and dissolving. A **chemical change** results when a new substance is formed that is different from the original material(s). The research question is "Is it possible to distinguish between physical and chemical changes?" Physical changes can frequently be easily "undone" or reversed. Ice can be melted and refrozen. Clay can be formed into a different shape. However, chemical changes are often very difficult to reverse. The appearing of a new and different substance is **proof** that a chemical change has occurred. There are some common **evidences** that often accompany chemical reactions. They are summarized as follows:

Evidence	Proof
A solid separates from a liquid.	The appearance of a new and different
A gas is produced.	substance is established by analytical tests.
The colors of the chemicals change permanently.	
The temperature of the substances changes.	
Light or sound is produced.	

These **evidences** alone do not prove that a chemical change has occurred. Some of these also accompany certain physical changes. For example, boiling water produces gas and sound during a phase change—a physical change. The appearance of solid crystalline salt in a slowly evaporating salt solution is another example of a physical change. In order to prove that a chemical change has taken place, the suspected new substance must be chemically analyzed in the laboratory to determine its identity. We will discuss chemical changes in greater detail in Chapter 9.

Pre-Laboratory Questions

Read the entire investigation. Answer the following questions prior to class on a separate sheet of paper. Use complete sentences.

1. What is a physical change?

2. What is a chemical change?

3. What are the evidences that a chemical change has occurred?

4. How can you prove that a chemical change has occurred?

5. State the research question.

6. For your hypothesis, state whether the following procedures will result in a chemical or a physical change:

   a. Burning sugar

   b. Mixing salt and water

   c. Mixing baking soda and vinegar

   d. Stretching a rubber band

   e. Mixing red cabbage juice and ammonia

   f. Mixing Epsom salts and ammonia

Procedures

A. Burning Sugar

1. Obtain a 15 × 15 cm (approximate) piece of aluminum foil.

2. Make a spoonlike instrument from the foil with a handle and a bowl to hold the sugar.

3. Write a description of the sugar in the first column of Table 1 in the Results section.

4. Light the Bunsen burner. Your teacher can show you how to use the burner and the lighter.

5. Place about 3 cm³ ($\frac{1}{2}$ tsp.) of sugar in the "bowl" at the end of the foil.

6. Hold the foil bowl over the flame. Tip the Bunsen burner slightly to make sure the sugar comes in direct contact with the flame. Make sure you don't spill any grains of sugar into the barrel of the burner. **Caution:** If the burner flares up, immediately put the burner down and ask for assistance.

7. When the sugar starts to burn, remove it from the flame.

8. After the flame dies, allow the sugar and foil to cool (about one minute).

9. Record your observations in Table 1. Include observations such as the production of heat, light, gas, or smoke, and any color changes and other physical changes. Then determine whether this was a chemical or a physical change.

10. Place the cooled foil and burned sugar residue in the trash.

B. Mixing Salt and Water

1. Write a description of the salt in the table.

2. Pour about 25 mL of tap water into the 250 mL beaker.

3. Add about 5 cm^3 (1 tsp.) of salt to the water and stir until dissolved.

4. Is there any evidence of a chemical change? Record your observations.

5. Place the beaker on the wire gauze on the tripod over the Bunsen burner.

6. Light the burner and boil the solution until all the water is gone (about 10-15 min.). Perform Section C of the investigation while the water is heating.

7. After the water has boiled away, turn off the Bunsen burner and observe what is left in the beaker.

8. Rinse the beaker with water in the sink.

C. Mixing Baking Soda and Vinegar

1. Write a description of the baking soda and vinegar in the table.

2. Pour about 25 mL of vinegar into a beaker.

3. Add about 5 cm^3 (1 tsp.) of baking soda to the vinegar.

4. Touch the base of the beaker with the back of your hand and note any temperature change. Record your observations and determination of the type of change in the table.

5. Discard the contents down the drain.

D. Stretching a Rubber Band

1. Write a description of the rubber band in the table.

2. Place the rubber band against your skin just under your lower lip. Notice the temperature of the rubber band.

3. Rapidly stretch the rubber band several times to its full extension. While it is fully extended, place it against your lower lip. Note any temperature change.

4. Record your observations and determination of type of change in the table.

E. Mixing Red Cabbage Extract and Ammonia

1. Write a description of the cabbage extract and ammonia in the table.

2. Place about 25 mL of cabbage extract in a 100 mL beaker.

3. Rinse the graduated cylinder with tap water and then add about 5 mL of ammonia to the cabbage extract. Record your observations in the table.

Chemical and Physical Changes

4. Flush the mixture down the drain with plenty of water and thoroughly rinse the beaker.

5. (Optional) Repeat steps 2 through 4 using 10 mL of vinegar in place of the ammonia.

F. Mixing Epsom Salts and Ammonia

1. Write a description of the saturated Epsom salts solution in the table.

2. Pour about 25 mL of the Epsom salts solution in a 100 mL beaker.

3. Add about 10 mL of ammonia to the Epsom salts solution. Record your observations and determination of type of change in the table.

4. Flush the mixture down the sink with plenty of water. Thoroughly rinse the beaker and dry it.

G. Cleanup

Unless your teacher directs otherwise, wash and dry all glassware thoroughly. Place all similar equipment together in one place. Return all chemicals and solutions to their designated locations. Be sure all bottle caps are tight. Lab cleanup should be considered part of every laboratory exercise.

Results

Table 1: Chemical and Physical Changes

	Describe Original Substances	New Substance (Yes/No)	Color Change (Yes/No)	Temp. Change (Yes/No)	Gas Produced (Yes/No)	Chemical or Physical Change?
Burning sugar						
Mixing salt and water						
Baking soda and vinegar						
Stretching a rubber band						
Cabbage extract and ammonia						
Epsom salts and ammonia						
Cabbage extract and vinegar (opt.)						

Discussion Questions

1. What is a physical change? Give four examples. _____

_____

_____

2. What is proof that a chemical change has occurred? _____

_____

_____

3. What are the evidences that a chemical change has occurred? _____

_____

_____

_____

4. In general terms, what is the difference between evidence and proof?

_____

_____

_____

5. Give an example from this investigation of a physical change producing evidence of a chemical change. _____

_____

6. Identify each of the following as a physical or a chemical change:

   a. Making ice cubes _____

   b. Coals burning in a barbecue _____

   c. Meat cooking _____

   d. A pencil being sharpened _____

   e. Sugar dissolving in water _____

   f. Gunpowder exploding _____

   g. Paper being folded _____

   h. Gasoline evaporating _____

   i. Gasoline burning _____

4B INVESTIGATION
Finding Absolute Zero

Name _____

Date_____ Hour_____

Objectives

The purpose of this investigation is to:

1. Demonstrate Charles's law.

2. Experimentally determine absolute zero, using the temperature range available in the laboratory.

Materials

Graph paper
Ice
Salt

Equipment

Beakers (600 mL) (2)
Beaker tongs
Bunsen burner
Burner lighter
Metric ruler
Stirring rod
Syringe (50 cm^3 with cap)
Test tube clamp
Thermometer (2)
Tripod or support stand with ring
Wire gauze

Introduction

Temperature is a measure of the average molecular kinetic energy. **Absolute zero** is the lowest theoretical temperature. It is thermodynamically impossible to reach absolute zero, although scientists have come within billionths of a degree of that elusive point. Scientists are not sure what might occur at that temperature, but it is assumed that all molecular motion and subatomic particle movement within atoms would cease. Some matter very near absolute zero (-273.15 °C) can change into another state called the Bose-Einstein Condensate (BEC).

How can absolute zero be determined if you cannot reach it? The original method was performed by a French physicist named Jacques Charles. Through experimentation, he discovered that the ratio of the volume of a gas and its Kelvin temperature is constant if the amount of gas and pressure are held constant. This relationship, known as **Charles's law,** is expressed by the equation

$$\frac{V_1}{T_1} = \frac{V_2}{T_2}$$

(NOTE: In the equation, the subscript 1 refers to the original condition of volume and temperature, while the subscript 2 refers to the new or final volume and temperature.) In other words, as the motion of the molecules slows down, the volume of the gas gets smaller (at constant pressure). Theoretically, this continues until the motion of the molecule stops and the volume becomes zero. (This is actually impossible for several reasons that you will learn in more advanced physical science courses.) Charles plotted a number of points on a graph comparing volume (on the vertical axis) and temperature (on the horizontal axis) for a sample of gas at constant pressure. He then extended a straight line through these plotted points until it reached zero volume. The temperature at which this occurs is absolute zero. This process of extending a relation beyond the range of available data to make a prediction is called **extrapolation.**

Pre-Laboratory Questions

Read the entire investigation. Answer the following questions prior to class on a separate sheet of paper. Use complete sentences.

1. What is believed to happen to molecules at absolute zero?

2. Why is absolute zero only a theoretical number?

3. State Charles's law in words and in a formula.

4. Through what standard method can absolute zero be estimated?

5. State the research question.

6. State your hypothesis.

Procedures

A. Establishing the Initial Syringe Volume

1. Pull the cap off the syringe tip and pull out the plunger so that the syringe contains 20 cm^3 of air.

2. Replace the cap back on the syringe and **do not remove it** during the rest of the investigation.

3. Record the room temperature in the data table in Results. (If you are observing SDs, record to the appropriate precision.)

4. Pour about 400 mL of water into a 600 mL beaker.

5. Assemble the tripod and wire gauze and place the beaker on the wire gauze. Light the burner, obtain a proper flame, and begin heating the water to about 90°C. Monitor the temperature with a thermometer.

   Do not exceed 95°C or cause the water to boil. Do not record the temperature until Part C.

B. Low Temperature Measurement

1. While heating the water, fill another 600 mL beaker about half full with ice.

2. In a second beaker, dissolve about 15 cm^3 (1 tbsp.) of salt in 500 mL of water. Pour the saltwater mixture over the ice until the beaker is about three-fourths full of water. The salt will keep the temperature of the ice water at or below 0°C.

3. Place another thermometer in the ice water and stir the water with a stirring rod (NOT the thermometer!) until the temperature is about 0°C.

5. Immerse the syringe in the ice water so that the entire syringe barrel is covered by water.

6. While the syringe is in the water, **slightly** push the plunger in every minute for three minutes to ensure that it is not sticking.

7. After you have pushed the plunger the third time, record the volume of the gas. Lift the syringe out of the water only enough to read the volume. You may be able to take the reading through the side of the beaker.

   This reading is the Low volume: _____ cm^3.

8. Immediately pull the plunger out **slightly** and read the volume.

   This reading is the High volume: _____ cm^3.

9. Calculate the average for the Low and High volumes: V_{avg} = _____ cm^3.

10. Record the average volume and the temperature from the cold water in the data table.

C. High Temperature Measurement

1. Using beaker tongs or a hot mitt, place the beaker with the hot water on the table and turn off the burner.

2. Submerge the syringe barrel in the hot water.

3. Use a test tube clamp to lift the plunger of the syringe out of the hot water. Keep the barrel submerged. Repeat steps 6 through 10 of Part B, except **pull** the plunger slightly three times. Record the High volume after three minutes.

   High volume: _____ cm^3

4. Immediately push the plunger in **slightly** and read the volume.

   Low volume: _____ cm^3

5. Calculate the average for the Low and High volumes: V_{avg} = _____ cm^3.

6. Record the average volume and the temperature from the hot water in the data table.

Results

A. Tabulated Data

Data Table: Charles's Law

Condition	$T(°C)$ x-axis	$V_{avg}(cm^3)$ y-axis
Cold		
Room		
Hot		

B. General Rules for Creating a Graph

1. Use a pencil.

2. Give the graph a title. Center it at the top of the graph on the paper.

3. Determine the independent variable (e.g., temperature) and the dependent variable (e.g., volume).

4. Name the x-axis with the independent variable and the y-axis with the dependent variable. Include the symbol and the units with the name, for example, "Temperature, T (°C)."

5. Select the appropriate size units so that you fill each axis as much as possible without creating gridline markings that are difficult to use. Make the graphing area as large as possible. Mark the axes indicating the intervals.

6. Use a ruler to draw the axes and other straight lines.

C. Finding Absolute Zero

1. Use one piece of 1/8- or 1/10-inch ruled graph paper or tape two pieces of 1/4-inch ruled graph paper together end to end.

2. Use the long dimension of the graph for the x-axis, which will represent temperature. Make the temperature in intervals of 5 or 10°C from −325°C to 100°C.

3. Mark the y-axis in intervals of 1 cm^3 from 0 to 25 cm^3.

4. Plot the three pairs of coordinates from the data table on the graph paper.

5. Lay a ruler on the graph paper so that it lies as close as possible to all of the points. The points probably will not lie on a single line; therefore, adjust the ruler so that the straight edge passes through one point and "splits the difference" between the other two. Draw a single straight line along the ruler.

6. Extend the line until it crosses the x-axis. Note that the y-coordinate (volume) at this point is 0 cm^3.

7. What is the temperature when the volume is zero? This is your estimate of absolute zero.

Discussion Questions

1. According to Charles's law, what happens to the volume of a gas as it is heated? _____

2. According to Charles's law, what happens to the volume of a gas as it is cooled? _____

3. Explain why it is dangerous to store aerosol cans in extremely hot places.

_____

_____

_____

4. Convert your room temperature from °C to K (K = °C + 273).

   T_{room} = _____

5. Recall from Charles's law that the ratio for a constant amount of gas at a constant pressure is V/T. Substituting the room-temperature values for V and T, find the volume-temperature ratio for your air sample.

$$\frac{V_{room}}{T_{room}} = \frac{\_\_\_\_\_cm^3}{\_\_\_\_\_K} = \frac{cm^3}{_____K}$$

This means that the volume will change by _____ cm^3 for every _____ K.

6. If the original 20.0 cm³ volume of air at room temperature (T_1) is heated to _____ °C (enter T_2—the recorded temperature of the hot water), determine the expected or theoretical volume in the syringe.

   a. Determine the change in temperature (ΔT): $T_2 - T_1 =$ _____ °C.
   Recall that Celsius degrees and Kelvins are the same "size," so $\Delta T =$ _____ K.

   b. A one Kelvin increase will cause a _____ cm³ increase in volume (from question 5).

   c. A two Kelvin increase will cause a _____ cm³ increase in volume.

   d. A (ΔT, from 6a) _____ Kelvin increase will cause a _____ cm³ increase in volume (ΔV).

   e. The theoretical volume of gas at T_2 will be the sum of the original volume (20.0 cm³) and ΔV.

   Calculated volume at T_2 _____

   Measured volume at T_2 (V_{avg}) _____ (See data table.)

Experimental Evaluation

7. Ideally, the three data points should lie on a straight line. Explain why they did not. _____

   _____

   _____

8. If a person could have used very accurate instruments, do you think that person could get the data points to fit exactly on a straight line? Explain

   _____

   _____

   _____

   _____

   _____

9. Besides using more accurate instruments, give two ways this experiment could be improved. _____

   _____

   _____

   _____

10. Did this experiment demonstrate the exact value of absolute zero? Explain.

   _____

   _____

   _____

11. (Optional) Some scientists think that absolute zero is not obtainable. Can you give a reason for this belief? _____

_____

_____

_____

Elements

Objective

The purpose of this demonstration is to familiarize you with the appearance and use of selected elements.

Materials

Selected element samples

Equipment

Periodic table

MSDS file or data forms (Optional)

Introduction

As you learned from your textbook, elements are the building blocks of all substances. All pure substances are either elements or compounds. Compounds can be broken down into their elements, but elements cannot be broken down any further without changing them into other elements. We will be observing a number of elements and noting their similarities and differences.

Prior to participating in this demonstration, you should review the material from Investigation 1A: "Laboratory Safety." You may be asked to complete this exercise as homework.

Pre-Laboratory Questions

Read the entire investigation. Answer the following questions prior to class on a separate sheet of paper. Use complete sentences.

1. What is the key difference between elements and compounds?

2. What would happen if an element were broken down any further?

3. What is the range of possible numbers for a hazard index?

4. What standard protective equipment should be used in a laboratory when handling unfamiliar chemicals?

Procedure

As each element is presented (or at each station around the room), write the name of the element in the blank provided in each section below. As time permits, find the element's symbol and its atomic number on the periodic table on pages 144 and 145 in your textbook, but do not delay observing the characteristics of the elements to do this during the demonstration. If the sample can be handled, note its hardness, texture, how crystalline it is, relative density, color, state, smell, and so on. (DO NOT TASTE ANY SUBSTANCE IN A LABORATORY!) If the element is in a sealed container, describe those properties that can be observed without opening the container. **Do not shake**

liquids. If the element is transparent, observe what it does to light, if anything. If the element has been artificially processed or formed, do not describe its man-made properties (e.g., spherical shape of lead shot).

You may also be required to note the safety information for each element using MSDS or other sources provided by your teacher. Fill this information in on copies of the blank MSDS form found in the back of this lab manual. Staple all pages together when you are finished.

A. Element _____ Symbol _____ Atomic Number _____

a. State
b. Hardness
c. Color
d. Relative density
e. Smell
f. Appearance—Circle all that are appropriate.

Transparent   Translucent

Opaque   Metallic

Crystalline/Faceted   Fibrous

Dusty/Sandy/Particles   Other: _____

B. Element _____ Symbol _____ Atomic Number _____

a. State
b. Hardness
c. Color
d. Relative density
e. Smell
f. Appearance—Circle all that are appropriate.

Transparent   Translucent

Opaque   Metallic

Crystalline/Faceted   Fibrous

Dusty/Sandy/Particles   Other: _____

C. Element _____ Symbol _____ Atomic Number _____

a. State
b. Hardness
c. Color
d. Relative density
e. Smell
f. Appearance—Circle all that are appropriate.

      Transparent   Translucent

         Opaque   Metallic

      Crystalline/Faceted   Fibrous

     Dusty/Sandy/Particles   Other: _____

D. Element _____ Symbol _____ Atomic Number _____

a. State
b. Hardness
c. Color
d. Relative density
e. Smell
f. Appearance—Circle all that are appropriate.

      Transparent   Translucent

         Opaque   Metallic

      Crystalline/Faceted   Fibrous

     Dusty/Sandy/Particles   Other: _____

E. Element _____ Symbol _____ Atomic Number _____

a. State
b. Hardness
c. Color
d. Relative density
e. Smell
f. Appearance—Circle all that are appropriate.

      Transparent   Translucent

         Opaque   Metallic

      Crystalline/Faceted   Fibrous

     Dusty/Sandy/Particles   Other: _____

F. Element _____ Symbol _____ Atomic Number _____

a. State
b. Hardness
c. Color
d. Relative density
e. Smell

f. Appearance—Circle all that are appropriate.
 	
    Transparent   Translucent
 	
        Opaque   Metallic
 	
    Crystalline/Faceted   Fibrous
 	
    Dusty/Sandy/Particles   Other: _____

G. Element _____ Symbol _____ Atomic Number _____

a. State
b. Hardness
c. Color
d. Relative density
e. Smell

f. Appearance—Circle all that are appropriate.
 	
    Transparent   Translucent
 	
        Opaque   Metallic
 	
    Crystalline/Faceted   Fibrous
 	
    Dusty/Sandy/Particles   Other: _____

H. Element _____ Symbol _____ Atomic Number _____

a. State
b. Hardness
c. Color
d. Relative density
e. Smell

f. Appearance—Circle all that are appropriate.
 	
    Transparent   Translucent
 	
        Opaque   Metallic
 	
    Crystalline/Faceted   Fibrous
 	
    Dusty/Sandy/Particles   Other: _____

Name _____

Date _____ Hour _____

I. Element _____ Symbol _____ Atomic Number _____

a. State	
b. Hardness	
c. Color	
d. Relative density	
e. Smell	

f. Appearance—Circle all that are appropriate.

Transparent   Translucent

Opaque   Metallic

Crystalline/Faceted   Fibrous

Dusty/Sandy/Particles   Other: _____

J. Element _____ Symbol _____ Atomic Number _____

a. State	
b. Hardness	
c. Color	
d. Relative density	
e. Smell	

f. Appearance—Circle all that are appropriate.

Transparent   Translucent

Opaque   Metallic

Crystalline/Faceted   Fibrous

Dusty/Sandy/Particles   Other: _____

K. Element _____ Symbol _____ Atomic Number _____

a. State	
b. Hardness	
c. Color	
d. Relative density	
e. Smell	

f. Appearance—Circle all that are appropriate.

Transparent   Translucent

Opaque   Metallic

Crystalline/Faceted   Fibrous

Dusty/Sandy/Particles   Other: _____

5B TEACHER DEMONSTRATION

Compounds

Objective

The purpose of this investigation is to demonstrate that the physical properties of a compound are different from the properties of the elements of which it is composed.

Materials

Baking soda—$NaHCO_3$
Calcium chloride—$CaCl_2$
Copper(II) sulfate—$CuSO_4$
Epsom salts—$MgSO_4$
Lead dioxide—PbO_2
Mercury(II) chloride—$HgCl_2$
Sodium chloride—$NaCl$
Vinegar—$C_2H_4O_2$

Equipment

Beakers, 100 mL (8)

Introduction

The **Law of Definite Composition** states that atoms of elements combine to form compounds in specific ratios. No matter where a compound is found, it always has the same composition with the same ratio of elements. The relationship between elements and compounds is similar to the relationship between letters and words. Words can be broken down into individual letters, but letters cannot be meaningfully broken down any further. It is only if letters are combined in specific ways that they form words with unique properties (meanings). Just as a word has properties different from the letters of which it is composed, a compound can have chemical and physical properties that are very different from the elements that make it up. For example, mercury(II) oxide (HgO) is composed of the two elements mercury and oxygen. Mercury is a liquid, silvery, toxic metal; and oxygen is a colorless, breathable gas that causes flammability in other substances. The compound mercury(II) oxide, however, is a bright orange solid powder. Its physical properties are totally different from the constituent elements.

You read in your book that sodium chloride is a harmless compound composed of two dangerous elements. However, combining toxic elements to form a compound does not always yield a harmless substance. This is particularly true of compounds containing heavy metals such as cadmium, mercury, and lead. Though their physical appearance may be quite different from their constituent elements, many compounds still require special handling and disposal procedures to protect people, animals, and the environment from harm.

Compounds

Procedures

As each compound is presented (or at each station around the room), describe its physical appearance, noting especially its color, state, and whether it is crystalline or powdery. Do not touch, taste, or shake the samples. On the subsequent lines, list the elements of which the compound is composed and summarize each element's physical properties from the information gathered in Teacher Demonstration 5A. The first one is done for you. You may also be required to note the safety information for each element using the MSDS or other sources provided by your teacher.

A. *Table Salt (NaCl)*   - White, crystalline solid, edible
Sodium   - Poisonous, soft reactive metal
Chlorine   - Greenish, poisonous gas

B. *Baking soda (NaHCO$_3$)*   - _____

_____   - _____

_____   - _____

_____   - _____

_____   - _____

C. *Epsom salts (MgSO$_4$)*   - _____

_____   - _____

_____   - _____

_____   - _____

D. Calcium chloride (CaCl₂) - _____

_____ - _____

_____ - _____

E. Copper (II) sulfate (CuSO₄) - _____

_____ - _____

_____ - _____

_____ - _____

F. Lead dioxide (PbO₂) - _____

_____ - _____

_____ - _____

G. Mercuric chloride (HgCl₂) - _____

_____ - _____

_____ - _____

H. Vinegar (C₂H₄O₂) - _____

_____ - _____

_____ - _____

_____ - _____

Discussion Questions

1. Explain what happens when the two hazardous elements sodium and chlorine are combined? _____

   _____

2. Do you think that you should dispose of lead and mercury compounds in the sink? _____

   _____

3. Why are mercury thermometers rarely used in the laboratory? _____

   _____

5. The formula for copper(II) sulfate is _____. One formula unit of this compound contains a total of _____ atoms: _____ atom(s) of copper, _____ atom(s) of sulfur, and _____ atom(s) of oxygen.

6. In the compound lead dioxide (PbO₂), the ratio of the number of Pb atoms to O atoms is _____ to _____.

5C INVESTIGATION

Mixtures

Name _____

Date _____ Hour_____

Objectives

The purpose of this investigation is to

1. Understand the differences between compounds and mixtures.

2. Demonstrate that the substances that make up a mixture retain their physical properties.

3. Separate a mixture based on the physical properties of its constituent substances.

Materials

Aluminum foil
Distilled water
Ice
Iron filings (15 cm^3 or 1 tbsp)
Orange juice, pulp free (75 mL)
Salt (15 cm^3 or 1 tbsp)
Sand (15 cm^3 or 1 tbsp)

Equipment

Beaker, 500 mL
Beakers, 100 mL (2)
Beaker, 50 mL
Bunsen burner
Burner lighter
Magnet
Microscope (low & 600+ power) (Optional)
Rubber band, wide
Rubber stoppers, small (3)
Stirring rod
Tripod
Wire gauze

Introduction

When two or more pure substances are combined without a subsequent chemical reaction, the result is called a **mixture.** These substances could be either elements or compounds. Mixtures differ from compounds in several ways. As you learned in Teacher Demonstration 5B, when elements react chemically to form a compound, the new substance often has physical properties that are different from those of the pure elements. In a mixture, each of the combined substances retains its original physical properties. Compounds and mixtures also differ in the method of separation of the original components. The elements in a compound have been combined chemically and have to be separated chemically. This requires energy in a form that will break the chemical bonds (usually heat or electricity). Mixtures, however, have undergone only a physical change. Often separating a mixture involves causing a phase change or using some physical process such as filtering. If heat is required to separate a mixture, the heat energy is not changing the composition of the substances; it is merely changing their state. The research question is "How can you separate the substances of a mixture?"

Many familiar materials are actually mixtures. Examples include air, salt water, paper, 14 kt. gold, steel, paint, chocolate, butter, ink, and concrete. Remember that mixtures can be combinations of either elements or compounds. A **homogeneous** mixture is one that is so well mixed that its appearance is the same throughout. Air, salt water, and 14 kt. gold are examples of homogeneous mixtures. No matter how small a sample you looked at, you could not visually tell the different substances apart. In a **heterogeneous** mixture, the parts can be visually identified or the particles are so different in size that they do not meet the definition of a homogeneous mixture. Concrete, composed of cement, sand, and gravel, is a good example of this kind of mixture. (Note that the composition of gravel is most likely a heterogeneous mixture as well.)

Pre-Laboratory Questions

Read the entire investigation. Answer the following questions prior to class on a separate sheet of paper. Use complete sentences.

1. What is a mixture composed of?

2. What kind of change is involved in separating a mixture?

3. What are two ways that mixtures differ from compounds?

4. What is the physical property of iron filings that allows it to be easily separated from its mixture in this investigation?

5. State the research question.

6. State a testable hypothesis concerning this investigation.

Procedures

A. Separating a mixture of iron filings, sand, and table salt

1. Mix the iron filings, sand, and table salt thoroughly together with the stirring rod in a 100 mL beaker. Note the appearance of the mixture.

2. Stir the mixture with the magnet. Periodically brush the iron filings off the magnet onto a piece of paper. Continue stirring the mixture with the magnet until no more iron filings adhere.

3. Add about 75 mL of distilled water to the beaker containing the sand and the salt and stir for two minutes to dissolve the salt.

4. Allow the sand to settle and carefully pour off as much of the salt water as possible into the second 100 mL beaker.

5. Light the Bunsen burner and place the *second* 100 mL beaker on the wire gauze on top of the tripod.

6. Heat the water to boiling and allow it to boil until almost all of the water has disappeared. Watch the beaker carefully. Remove the beaker from the flame just before the last of the water boils away. Allow the residual heat to evaporate the remaining water. Turn off the burner.

7. Discard the sand into the trash and wash both of the beakers. Place the iron filings in the designated receptacle.

B. Separating Water from Orange Juice

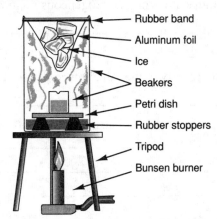

Rubber band
Aluminum foil
Ice
Beakers
Petri dish
Rubber stoppers
Tripod
Bunsen burner

1. Pour about 50 mL of the orange juice into the 500 mL beaker. The bottom should be covered with about 1 cm of fluid. Note the appearance of the orange juice.

2. Place the three rubber stoppers in the beaker, wide end down, in a triangular pattern.

3. Place a petri dish (or other flat support) on top of the rubber stoppers and place an empty 50 mL beaker on top of that positioned in the center of the large beaker.

4. Cover the mouth of the large beaker with aluminum foil making sure that there is a cone-shaped depression in the foil. Be sure that the tip of the depression is directly over the empty 50 mL beaker. Fasten the foil to the rim of the beaker with a rubber band.

5. Place three or four ice cubes in the depression in the foil.

6. Carefully place the large beaker on top of the wire gauze on the tripod.

7. Light the Bunsen burner underneath, placing the flame under the space between the stoppers, and gently heat the beaker.

8. Turn off the burner when 5-10 mL of liquid has dripped into the small beaker. Note the color of the liquid in the small beaker. It is not necessary to boil off all of the liquid in the large beaker.

9. Make sure that the beakers and other parts are thoroughly cleaned when you are finished.

C. Optional Observations

1. Following the instructions of your teacher, use a microscope to observe under low power a slide of the iron filing-salt-sand mixture. Note any differences among the particles you can see.

2. Observe under high power a microscope slide of a sample of orange juice. Note anything that might indicate the presence of more than one substance.

Discussion Questions

A. Separating Iron Filings, Sand, and Salt

1. Was this a homogeneous or a heterogeneous mixture? Explain. _____

    _____

    _____

2. What physical property of the salt allowed you to separate it from the sand?

    _____

3. How could you separate two substances such as sand and gravel that are not soluble in water? _____

    _____

    _____

B. Separating an Orange Juice Mixture

1. What was the appearance of the liquid in the small beaker? _____

    _____

2. What do you think it was? Where did it come from? _____

    _____

3. What was the function of the ice in the foil? _____

    _____

4. How does this demonstrate that orange juice is a mixture and not a compound? _____

    _____

5. Was the orange juice a homogeneous or a heterogeneous mixture? Explain.

    _____

    _____

    _____

    _____

    _____

Objectives

The purpose of this investigation is to

1. Illustrate the limitations of relying solely on your senses for scientific observations.

2. Attempt to identify two different elements by their flame test emissions.

Materials

Calcium chloride ($CaCl_2$)
Copper(II) chloride ($CuCl_2$)
Lithium chloride (LiCl)
Manganese chloride ($MnCl_2$)
Potassium chloride (KCl)
Sodium chloride (NaCl)
Strontium chloride ($SrCl_2$)
Wooden splints

Equipment

Bunsen burner
Safety glasses
Diffraction grating spectroscopes
   (optional)

Introduction

The electrons surrounding the nucleus of an atom exist in specific energy levels. When an element is heated, its electrons gain energy. If enough energy is added, an electron will jump to a higher energy level, called an excited state. This state is not stable, and the electron will immediately return to a lower energy level. When this happens, the excess energy is released as visible light or some other form of radiant energy. The wavelength of the light given off (its color) depends on the difference between the energy levels. Each element has a specific arrangement of electrons that can change energy levels in unique ways. As a result, each element gives off a distinctive set of wavelengths called an **emission spectrum.** This spectrum is unique to each element and can be used to identify it. If the emission spectrum contains several distinct wavelengths (bright line spectrum), they are often not apparent to the naked eye. For example, when an element is heated, it may appear to our eyes to glow orange; but if that orange light were dispersed by a prism, it could separate into several individual color bands. A **spectroscope** is a device that can disperse a beam of light into a spectrum.

A **spectrometer** is a laboratory instrument that displays the emission spectrum of a substance on a numerical scale and can give an accurate analysis of elemental composition. The composition of stars is determined by this very process.

Read the entire demonstration. Answer the following questions prior to class on a separate sheet of paper. Use complete sentences.

1. What happens to electrons when they gain energy?

2. What happens to the excess energy when the electrons return to lower energy levels?

3. What is an emission spectrum?

4. Explain why each element gives off a unique emission spectrum.

5. Why is the burner flame adjusted to eliminate the orange tip of the flame?

6. Why must a clean wood splint be used for each new sample?

Procedures

1. Observe as your teacher adjusts the burner flame to be nearly invisible or emitting only a blue glow.

2. Next, your teacher will dip a fresh, damp wood splint into a sample of each element, one at a time, and then place the element into the hottest part of the flame to produce the incandescent emission.

3. Record the color you observe in the table below. Be as descriptive as possible (e.g., write "red-orange" rather than just "orange"). This will establish your list of reference colors for the unknown samples.

4. Observe as your teacher tests two samples of unidentified elements in the flame. These unknowns are among those you have already observed. Record their colors in the table for Unknown I and II.

5. (Optional) Using a spectroscope, attempt to identify any bright lines in the spectra of selected elements as they are being tested. Record their colors and the number of lines of each, if applicable.

Results

Table: Emission Data

Element	Color	Bright Lines (Optional)
Calcium		
Copper		
Lithium		
Manganese		
Potassium		
Sodium		
Strontium		
Unknown I—		
Unknown II—		

Experimental Evaluation

1. Does the flame test as demonstrated provide evidence or proof of the identity of an element? Explain. _____

   _____

   _____

2. Why was it difficult to identify Unknown II? _____

   _____

3. Do you think that the elements that appeared to be the same color in the flame tests would show that same similarity if their emission spectra were analyzed? Explain. _____

   _____

   _____

4. What would you need to do to positively identify Unknown II? _____

   _____

Objective

The purpose of this investigation is to illustrate radioactive decay.

Materials

Pennies (or M&Ms™)

Introduction

From your textbook, you learned that some atoms undergo changes where their nuclei emit rays and/or particles in a process called radioactive decay. The rate at which this occurs varies among isotopes and is measured by the time it takes for one-half of a given isotope to decay to (be converted into) a different isotope. This interval is called the **half-life** and is unique to each isotope for a certain kind of decay. Suppose isotope A decays into isotope B with a half-life of one year. If you start with 100 g of isotope A, at the end of one year there will be about 50 g of isotope A and about 50 g of isotope B. In other words, each atom has a 50-50 (50%) chance of decaying during the first half-life. During the second half-life (the second year), each remaining atom of isotope A has a 50% chance of decaying again. At the end of two years, there will be about 25 g of isotope A left and about 75 g of isotope B. Why doesn't all of the remaining 50 g of isotope A decay during the second half-life? The principle of **independence** states that each event of radioactive decay is not affected by (is independent of) what has happened before. In other words, no matter how many half-lives have already passed, the chance that any of the remaining atoms will decay during the next half-life remains only 50%. In our example, at the end of three years, there will be about 12.5 g of isotope A remaining; at the end of four years, 6.25 g, and so on. You can see that even with a relatively short half-life of one year, it would take a long time for an isotope to be completely eliminated through radioactive decay. The concern that many people have about the safety of nuclear power facilities stems from the fact that much of the waste contains radioactive elements with very long half-lives emitting hazardous radiation.

Pre-Laboratory Questions

Read the entire investigation. Answer the following questions priot to class on a separate piece of paper. Use complete sentences.

1. Define the term *half-life*.

2. What does it mean to state that one event is independent of another?

3. Isotope A beta decays to isotope B and has a half-life of six months. If you begin with 500 g of isotope A, how much of each isotope will be present after six months, twelve months, and eighteen months?

Procedures

A. Using Penny Flips as a Model for Radioactive Decay

In this exercise, each penny will represent a radioactive atom. A flip represents the period of one half-life. Also, each flip of a penny, like each event of radioactive decay, is an independent event. This means that the chance of getting tails (50%) is not affected by the previous flip. If a person flips a penny five times and obtains five tails in a row, the chance of obtaining tails on the sixth flip is still only 50%.

1. Everyone in the class should obtain a penny. (For small classes, you may be asked to take two or more.) Record the total number of pennies in Table 1. This figure represents the initial number of "radioactive atoms."

2. At a signal from the teacher, everyone should flip his coin(s).

3. Record the number of heads and tails on the blackboard or on a sheet of paper.

4. The teacher will flip a penny, and the side showing will be noted. The students' pennies that had the same side showing as the teacher will represent the radioactive atoms that have decayed during the first half-life and should be removed. The affected pennies should not be flipped in any future trials.

5. Record the number of pennies remaining (undecayed) in Table 1 for half-life 1.

6. Repeat steps 2–5 with the remaining pennies until all the pennies have "decayed."

7. Plot your results on the blank graph provided. Carefully sketch a *smooth* curve through the data points. This curve is called a **decay curve.**

B. M&Ms (Alternative)

In this exercise, each M&M will represent a radioactive atom.

1. Place forty M&Ms in a box.

2. Cover the box and shake it briefly but vigorously.

3. Remove the cover and count the M&Ms that landed with the printed side up. These represent atoms that have decayed. Remove and eat them.

4. Record the number of M&Ms remaining in Table 2 for half-life 1.

5. Repeat steps 2–4 until all the M&Ms are gone. Each trial represents one half-life.

6. Plot your results on the blank graph provided. Carefully sketch a *smooth* curve through the data points. This curve is called a **decay curve.** (*Note:* If you are performing both experiments in this investigation, use a different color from the penny data.)

Results

Table 1: Radioactive Decay (Pennies)

Number of half-lives	Pennies Remaining
0	Initial _____
1	
2	
3	
4	
5	
6	
7	
8	
9	
10	

Table 2: Radioactive Decay (M&Ms)

Number of half-lives	M&Ms Remaining
0	40
1	
2	
3	
4	
5	
6	
7	
8	
9	
10	

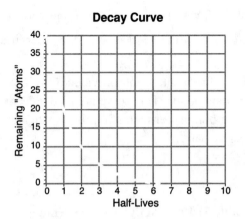

Decay Curve

Discussion Questions

1. The half-life of carbon-14 is about six thousand years, and carbon-14 decays to nitrogen-14. If an Egyptian mummy contained 10 g of carbon-14 when it was buried and now has 5 g, how old is the mummy? _____ How many grams of nitrogen-14 were produced during that time? _____ In another six thousand years, how much carbon-14 will remain? _____ What would be the total amount of nitrogen-14 produced in twelve thousand years after the burial of the mummy? _____

2. What is the chance that a carbon-14 atom will decay in six thousand years? _____ If that atom does not decay after six thousand years, what would be the chance of that atom decaying in the next six thousand years? Explain. _____

_____

_____

Experimental Evaluation

3. What was the chance of any of the "radioactive atoms " decaying during each trial? _____

4. If you performed a decay trial with fifty of your "atoms" (pennies or M&Ms), would you expect to obtain exactly twenty-five "decays"? Explain. _____

_____

_____

5. How many half-lives were needed to eliminate nearly all of the original "isotopes"? _____

_____

6. Based on your answer to question 5, if the hazardous radioactive isotope cobalt-60 has a half-life of five years, how long will it be until essentially all of the cobalt-60 has decayed away? _____

7. Describe the shape of your graphs. Discuss steepness of slope and relative height of the curve with increasing half-lives. _____

_____

_____

_____

8. (Optional) If you performed both of the experiments in this investigation, how do the shapes of the graphs compare? _____

_____

9. (Optional) What are some assumptions scientists must make when using radioactive decay to date ancient objects? _____

_____

_____

_____

_____

_____

_____

_____

7 INVESTIGATION
Metals and Nonmetals

Objective

The purpose of this investigation is to demonstrate the differing physical properties of metals, nonmetals, and metalloids.

Materials

Aluminum
Antimony
Bismuth
Carbon (coal)
Carbon (graphite, powdered, 15 cm³)
Carbon (soft drawing pencil
   [4B or softer])
Copper (wire)
Iodine crystals
Iron (nail)
Silicon
Sulfur
Wood (drawing pencil)

Equipment

Beaker (250 mL)
Beaker tongs or hot mitt
Bunsen burner
Electrical conductivity apparatus
   (see Investigation 2B)
Multimeter (if available)
Tripod
Wire gauze

Introduction

The elements on the periodic table can be divided into three classes: the metals, the nonmetals, and the metalloids. The periodic table in your textbook contains a stair-step dividing line between the metals and the nonmetals. The elements in green that are adjacent to the dividing line are called the metalloids. Not surprisingly, the three classes of elements have different physical properties. The question is "Can certain physical properties of an element be predicted based on its location on the periodic table?"

In this investigation we will examine a few physical properties of several metals, nonmetals, and metalloids. Because the elements in a class have similar electron structures, you would expect them to have similar properties as well. Most metals are solids, will easily conduct electricity and heat, are malleable, and have a silvery luster. Nonmetals may exist as solids, liquids, or gases, though the gaseous state is the most common. They generally do not conduct electricity or heat well, and the solids are brittle. Rather than having a silvery luster, nonmetals exist in a variety of colors. The metalloids are a third class that fall around the dividing line and will have some of the properties of each of the other classes. For example, antimony (Sb) is an extremely brittle metalloid. It has a metallic luster with a flaky, crystalline texture. It is bluish white and conducts heat and electricity poorly.

Not all of the elements have all of the properties that would be expected of their class. Because they all have different electron structures, the elements also differ in the degree to which they exhibit these properties. For example, a sterling silver spoon is malleable at room temperature and easily bent. Iron is also malleable, though it requires more vigorous pounding to deform it. Some metals are better conductors than others. Generally speaking, however, you can predict which physical properties an element will have based upon its location in the periodic table.

Pre-Laboratory Questions

Read the entire investigation. Answer the following questions prior to class on a separate sheet of paper. Use complete sentences.

1. Name the three classes into which the elements can be divided.

2. Name the four physical properties that we will be examining in this investigation.

3. What is distinctive about the metalloids?

4. State the research question.

5. For your hypothesis, first list each of the properties tested and then predict the results of your investigation on metals and nonmetals.

Procedures

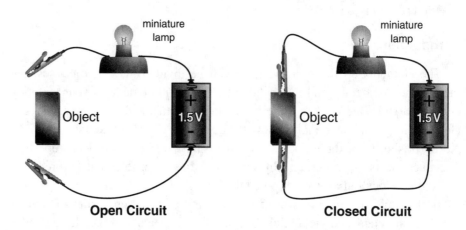

Open Circuit   **Closed Circuit**

A. Electrical Conductivity

1. Obtain the electrical conductivity apparatus described in Investigation 2B (or a multimeter, if available) and make the connections to the battery and the test leads, as applicable.

2. Touch the ends of the two wires together and observe whether the conductivity apparatus lamp lights. If the bulb does not light, check the connections between the wires, the battery, and the lamp base. This type of control ensures that your apparatus is functioning properly. (If using a multimeter, turn it on, select "Ω" or the resistance scale, and touch the test leads together. The display should show zero ohms [Ω])

3. Test the electrical conductivity of copper by touching the ends of the wires to the copper wire. Record the results in Table 1. (If using a multimeter, record the numerical value of the resistance in ohms.)

4. Repeat step 3 with the aluminum, antimony, bismuth, carbon (coal), iron, lead, silicon, sulfur, and the *wooden* part of the drawing pencil. The pencil will be considered a nonmetal in the conduction tests because it is composed mostly of carbon, hydrogen, and oxygen.

5. Test the conductivity of both the *graphite* portion of the drawing pencil and the powdered graphite. Record your results in Table 1.

6. If you are using a multimeter, you may assume that a reading less than 10 ohms indicates the material is a conductor. A reading over 10 ohms indicates a nonconductor.

7. Clean the test leads with a damp paper towel. Store the parts of the apparatus for future use when finished. (Turn off the multimeter.)

B. Conduction of Heat

1. Pour about 150 mL of water into a 250 mL beaker.

2. Place the beaker on the wire gauze on the tripod, light the Bunsen burner, and heat the water to a near boil; then turn off the burner.

3. Using beaker tongs or another method of protection, carefully remove the beaker from the tripod.

4. Twist four 8 cm lengths of uninsulated copper wire together. Place the resulting wire bundle, the iron nail, and the pencil into the beaker so that their ends protrude out of the water.

5. After three minutes, carefully touch the upper ends of the wire bundle, the nail, and the pencil. Based on how warm they feel, record whether each is a good heat conductor in Table 2.

C. Malleability

Compare the flexibility of a copper wire, an iron nail, and a pencil. Record your results in Table 2.

D. Physical Appearance

Observe the color and luster of the elements listed in Table 3.

E. Cleanup

When finished, return all materials and equipment to their designated locations. If graphite was spilled, carefully clean it up with soap and water. Pour out the water and dry the beaker.

Results

Table 1: Conduction of Electricity

Substance	Metal/Nonmetal/ Metalloid	Conductivity (Y/N)
Aluminum		
Antimony		
Bismuth		
Carbon (coal)		
Graphite (pencil)		
Graphite (powdered)		
Copper		
Iron		
Lead		
Silicon		
Sulfur		
Wood		

Table 2: Heat Conduction and Malleability

Substance	Metal/ Nonmetal	Conduction of Heat (Good/Poor)	Malleable (Y/N)
Copper			
Iron			
Wood			

Table 3: Appearance

Substance	Metal/Nonmetal/ Metalloid	Color	Metallic Luster (Y/N)
Aluminum			
Antimony			
Bismuth			
Carbon (graphite)			
Copper			
Iodine			
Iron			
Lead			
Silicon			
Sulfur			

Discussion Questions

Use complete sentences for your answers.

1. Did the results of your investigation match the predictions you made in your hypothesis? _____

   _____

   _____

2. Would you expect the measurable physical properties of different metals (such as conductivity, hardness, malleability, etc.) to be exactly the same? Explain why or why not. _____

   _____

   _____

3. Give an example from this investigation of two metals that showed a difference in a physical property. _____

   _____

4. You were told that nonmetals do not conduct electricity. You tested one nonmetal that in one form *was* a conductor. Name the element and which form conducted. _____

   _____

5. If it were available, why would you not be able to test fluorine for the physical properties checked in this investigation? _____

   _____

   _____

   _____

6. Name the metalloids that you tested for electrical conductivity. Based on their appearance, what would you predict about their malleability? Why?

   _____

   _____

   _____

   _____

7. Which parts of computers are formed principally from silicon? _____

   _____

   _____

Name _____

Date _____ Hour _____

Objectives

The purpose of this exercise is to provide practice in

1. Determining the electron transfers and ionization state during the formation of selected ions.

2. Drawing electron dot diagrams for selected elements.

3. Drawing electron dot diagrams for selected ionic compounds.

Instructions

Review Section 8A in your textbook. Complete the following statements by supplying the appropriate word(s) or numerical answer(s). Note in your textbook that ionic charges are written with the number first followed by the sign.

1. What is an ion? _____

For questions 2–7, the statements indicate how the atom will become ionized as it bonds ionically.

2. Potassium (Z = 19) has _____ valence electron(s). Potassium will _____ (lose/gain) _____ electron(s), resulting in an ion with a charge of _____ .

3. Calcium (Z = 20) has _____ valence electron(s). Calcium will _____ (lose/gain) _____ electron(s), resulting in an ion with a charge of _____ .

4. Oxygen (Z = 8) has _____ valence electron(s). Oxygen will _____ (lose/gain) _____ electron(s), resulting in a charge of _____ .

5. Bromine (Z = 35) has _____ valence electron(s). Bromine will _____ (lose/gain) _____ electron(s), resulting in an ion with a charge of _____ .

6. The oxygen (Z = 8) ion, O^{2-}, has _____ protons and _____ electrons.

7. The magnesium (Z = 12) ion, Mg^{2+}, has _____ protons and _____ electrons.

8. Give the following information about a neutral atom of Krypton-84 (Z = 36).

The number of electrons in each energy level _____

_____

The atomic number _____

The number of protons _____

The number of electrons _____

The mass number _____

The number of neutrons _____

For problems 9 and 10, practice arranging the dots in the order shown on page 167 of your textbook.

9. Draw the electron dot diagrams for the following elements using their symbols given below.

Na   Ca   Ar   K   S   Cl

10. Draw the electron dot diagrams to represent the steps in ionic bonding. Follow the example given for CaS.

Example:

a. KI

b. NaBr

c. $CaCl_2$

Objectives

The purpose of this exercise is to

1. Reinforce the concepts of covalent bonding you have learned.

2. Understand the restrictions that limit the number of covalent bonds in a compound.

Introduction

You have learned from your textbook and Applications 8A that elements with very different electronegativities form compounds by transferring electrons. Elements with nearly full (nonmetals) and nearly empty (metals) valence energy levels are able to bond to each other in this way. When nonmetals form a bond, however, there are two reasons electron transfer does not occur. Transferring all of a typical nonmetal's valence electrons would give the other nonmetal far more than the required eight electrons to meet the octet rule. In addition, the electronegativity of the nonmetal would not be strong enough to retain the extra electrons even if it could take them. Therefore, when nonmetal atoms (having similar electronegativities) form bonds, they must share just enough electrons with other atoms to complete their valence level. This is called **covalent bonding**. In this exercise we will use "jigsaw puzzle" models to illustrate the way that atoms form single covalent bonds with other atoms. (*Note:* Due to the limitations of the models, you will not be able to make double or triple bonds.) Recall that a covalent bond consists of a pair of electrons shared by two atoms. In this exercise, you will "build" a number of covalent molecules and you will learn why some covalent molecules (and their compounds) cannot exist.

Procedures

1. Cut out the puzzle pieces found on page 100. The dots on the models represent valence electrons. Using these pieces, construct the molecules listed in Table 1. Arrange the pieces so that there are two electrons around hydrogen and eight around each of the other elements. The diatomic element hydrogen (H_2) is shown as an example below.

2. Once you have constructed each molecule from the puzzle pieces, draw its electron dot structure in the right-hand column of Table 1.

Table 1: Electron Dot Models

Compound	Electron Dot Structure
Cl_2	
CH_4	
CCl_4	
NH_3	
C_2H_6	
CH_2Cl_2	
(Give an alternate arrangement.)	

3. Attempt to construct the molecules of the compounds listed in Table 2. Not all of the compounds are valid because their molecules cannot be formed. Write *Y* in the blank if a valid molecule can be formed and *N* if it cannot.

Table 2: Molecular Validity

Formula	Valid? (Y/N)	Formula	Valid? (Y/N)
H_3		$HCNOH_4$	
HCl		$NHCl_2$	
CH_3		NH_4	
NCl_4		C_2H_5OH	
$CHCl_3$		CH_3Cl_2	

Discussion Questions

1. What are valence electrons? _____

_____

2. What is the octet rule? _____

_____

3. Name an element that is an exception to the octet rule. _____

_____

4. Why is the element in question #3 an exception? _____

_____

5. What is a covalent bond and why does it form? _____

_____

_____

6. How is a covalent bond different from an ionic bond? _____

_____

7. Does the electron dot diagram of a molecule show all of its electrons? Explain your answer. _____

_____

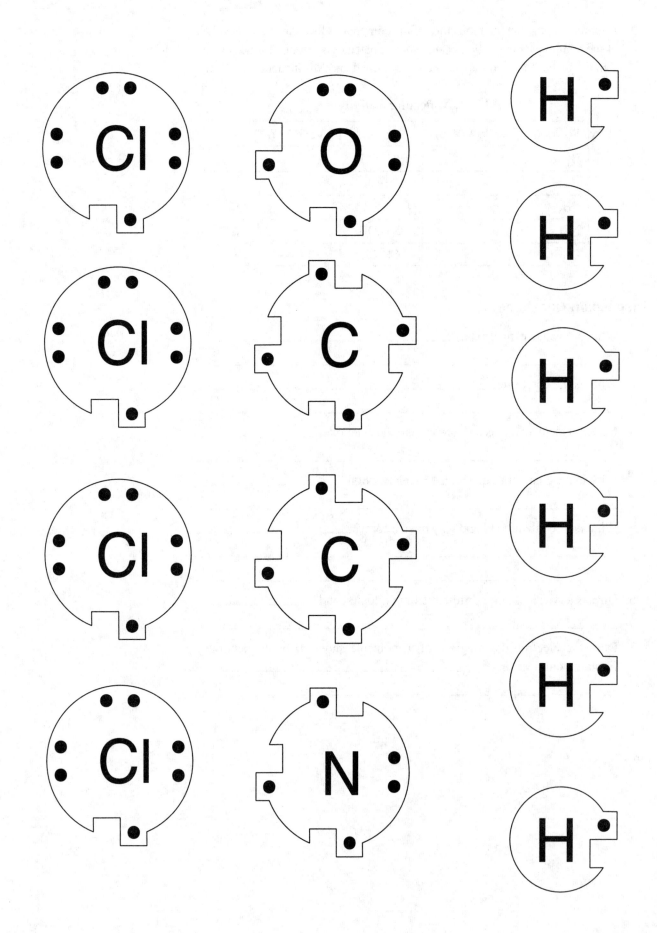

8C APPLICATIONS

Bonding Summary

Name _____

Date_____   Hour_____

Objective

The purpose of this exercise is to provide additional review of covalent and ionic bonding concepts.

Questions

1. A bond that results from the transfer of electrons between two or more atoms is called a(n) _____ bond.

2. A bond that results from the sharing of electrons between two or more atoms is called a(n) _____ bond.

3. The type of bond that usually forms between two nonmetal atoms is called a(n) _____ bond.

4. The type of bond that usually forms between metal and nonmetal atoms is called a(n) _____ bond.

5. Sulfur (Z = 16) has _____ valence electron(s). Sulfur can gain or share _____ electrons.

6. Hydrogen (Z = 1) has _____ valence electron(s). Hydrogen can gain or share _____ electron(s).

7. When sulfur and hydrogen react together, one sulfur atom will combine with _____ hydrogen atom(s).

8. Give the following information for arsenic-75.

    Atomic number: _____

    Number of protons: _____

    Number of electrons: _____

    Number of electrons in each energy level: 1st Level—_____, 2nd Level—_____, 3rd Level—_____, 4th Level—_____

    Mass number: _____

    Number of neutrons: _____

Diagrams

1. Draw the electron dot diagrams for the following neutral elements. Follow the dot sequence given on page 167 of your textbook.

Cl   Zn

P   Xe

Ge   Rb

2. Draw the electron dot diagrams to illustrate covalent bonding in the following compounds.

   a. N_2 b. H_2O

   c. C_2H_5OH (carbons go together)   d. O_2

3. Draw electron dot diagrams to illustrate the steps in ionic bonding for the following compounds.

   a. KF   b. MgS

Name _____

Date _____ Hour_____

Objective

The purpose of this investigation is to determine which types of bonds are present in some common materials by examining their electrical conductivities.

Materials

Baking soda
Brass (or some other metal)
Cola soft drink
Copper metal (wire or sheet)
Orange drink mix (e.g., Tang™)
Sugar
Table salt (NaCl)
Vegetable oil
Water (distilled)

Equipment

Beaker (250 mL)
Electrical conductivity apparatus
    assembled in Investigation 2B
Tablespoon

Introduction

You have learned from your study of chemical bonds that the type of bond often determines the physical properties of a material as well as its chemical properties. This fact was demonstrated in Investigation 7, "Metals and Nonmetals," where you compared appearance, electrical and thermal conductivity, and malleability of several different substances. You found that metals often have a similar appearance and good conductive characteristics, but the appearance of solid ionic and covalent compounds can vary greatly, and they generally conduct electricity poorly. The conductivity of the various types of bonds can be explained as follows:

Metals. Electricity is conducted through a substance by electrons or charged particles (ions) that are free to move around. The valence electrons of metals, whether in the solid or liquid (melted) state, are very mobile since they are not strongly attracted to any particular atom. This is a key principle of metallic bonding. Metals, therefore, conduct electricity in any state.

Ionic compounds. Ionic solids contain charged particles, but the crystal structure holds the ions in a fixed position. Since the charged particles cannot move, dry solid ionic compounds will not conduct electricity. However, if the ionic solid can dissolve in water or if the solid is melted, the charged particles separate from each other (dissociate) and become free to move. Consequently, an ionic compound dissolved in water or in the molten state will conduct electricity. Though polyatomic ions (HCO_3^-, for example) are held together with covalent bonds, the ions still carry charges and their solutions will conduct electricity.

Covalent compounds. Covalent compounds in an un-ionized state have neither free electrons nor charged particles and will not conduct electricity. Most covalent compounds will not form a solution with water while some are only poorly soluble. Other covalent compounds such as sugar are readily soluble in water. A few covalent compounds ionize in water, and these will conduct electricity as in the case of ionic compounds.

If you were given an unknown solid, how could you determine with fair confidence if it contained metallic, ionic, or covalent bonds? In this investigation, you will use the property of electrical conductivity to help evaluate the kinds of bonds in several substances.

The following table summarizes the electrical properties of compounds containing the different types of bonds.

Bonding Type	State	Conduction
Metallic	Solid metal	Yes
	Molten metal	Yes
Ionic	Crystalline solid	No
	Solution (water)	Yes
	Molten	Yes
Covalent	Solid	No
	Liquid	No
	Solution (water)	No (possibly yes)

Pre-Laboratory Questions

Read the entire investigation. Answer the following questions prior to class on a separate sheet of paper. Use complete sentences.

1. What test will we be using in this investigation to determine the type of bond?

2. Why do metals conduct electricity?

3. Under what conditions do ionic compounds conduct electricity? Explain why.

4. Why do covalent compounds not conduct electricity easily?

5. Is it possible to determine the type of bond in a substance by using conductivity alone?

6. State the research question.

7. State your hypothesis and predict the conductivity of the following materials, given their composition.

Substance	Composition
Baking soda	$NaHCO_3$
Brass	Cu, Zn alloy
Copper	Cu
Cola	primarily C, O, and H compounds
Orange drink mix	primarily C, O, and H compounds
Sugar	C, O, and H compound
Table salt	NaCl
Vegetable oil	primarily C, O, and H compounds
Water (distilled)	H_2O

Procedures

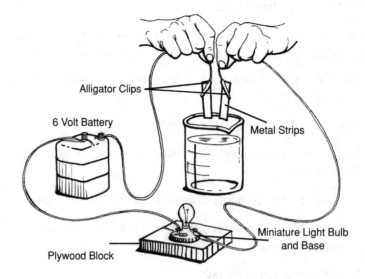

Alligator Clips

6 Volt Battery

Metal Strips

Miniature Light Bulb
and Base

Plywood Block

1. Obtain the parts for and assemble the electrical conductivity apparatus used in Investigation 2B. Since you will be testing solutions, the alligator clips and metal strips (probes) should be attached. Touch the two probes together to make sure that the light bulb works. If it doesn't light up, check all of the electrical connections.

2. Test the copper and the brass for conductivity by touching both probes to the surface of the solid. Record your results in the data table.

Note: Be sure to thoroughly clean and dry the probes and the beaker after each of the following liquid tests.

3. Test the four liquids (vegetable oil, cola, distilled water, and tap water) for conductivity, one at a time. Pour approximately 150 mL of the liquid into the 250 mL beaker. Test for conductivity by placing the probes in the liquid (do not let the probes touch each other). Record your results in the data table.

4. Put 30 cm³ (2 tablespoons) of baking soda in the dry beaker. Test the powder for conductivity by placing the probes in the material. Do not let the probes touch each other or the bottom of the beaker. Add 150 mL of distilled water to the dry material in the beaker and stir. After the baking soda is dissolved, test again for conductivity by placing the probes in the solution. Record your results for both the dry and the dissolved baking soda in the data table.

5. Repeat step 4 using table salt, sugar, and the orange drink mix. Record your results for both dry and dissolved materials in the data table.

6. In the third column write *M* if you believe metallic bonds are present, *I* if ionic, and *C* if covalent. If the test is inconclusive, write a question mark.

Name _____

Date_____   Hour_____

Results

Data Table: Properties of Compounds

Compound	Conducts? (Y/N)	Bond Type
Brass		
Copper		
Cola		
Vegetable oil		
Distilled water		
Tap water		
Baking soda powder		
Dissolved powder		
Table salt crystals		
Salt water solution		
Sugar crystals		
Sugar water solution		
Orange drink mix (dry)		
Orange drink (liquid)		

Discussion Questions

1. Why do ionic compounds not conduct electricity when they are in the crystalline solid state? _____

   _____

2. Fill in the following blanks with *metals* or *nonmetals*.

   a. Metallic bonds form between two elements that are _____.

   b. Ionic bonds form between _____ and _____.

   c. Covalent bonds form between two _____.

3. Predict the type of bond in each of the following compounds.

   a. CO_2 _____

   b. $MgCl_2$ _____

   c. LiCl   _____

   d. SO_2 _____

   e. Ni-Cu alloy _____

Experimental Evaluation

4. Your results for baking soda ($NaHCO_3$, sodium bicarbonate) should have showed that it contained ionic bonds.

   a. Name the cation (positive ion). _____

   b. Name the anion (negative ion). _____

5. What type of bonds exist between the atoms of the anion in question 4?

   _____

6. If the conductivity test demonstrates that a substance has ionic bonds, does this demonstrate that the substance does not have **any** covalent bonds? Explain. _____

7. If some of your covalently-bonded materials conducted electricity, how can you explain those observations? _____

_____

8. Suppose that during one of the tests the light bulb did not light up and you concluded that the material had covalent bonds. If you had not performed the bulb check at the beginning, how sure could you be of your results?

_____

_____

9. What does this tell you about the necessity of controls in a scientific experiment? _____

_____

Name _____

Date _____ Hour_____

Objectives

The purpose of this exercise is to

1. Provide practice in determining oxidation numbers for various elements.

2. Write correct compound formulas using the information gained from oxidation numbers.

Introduction

A chemical formula is an abbreviated way to represent the composition of a pure substance. It tells you which elements are part of the compound, as well as the actual number of atoms of each element that are present in a molecule of the compound. If the compound is ionic, then the formula gives the relative numbers of atoms of each element in the *formula unit*. For example, the chemical formula for the molecular compound water is H_2O. The subscript *2* reveals that there are two hydrogen atoms. The oxygen lacks a subscript, which indicates there is only one in the molecule. If a subscript follows parentheses containing part of the formula, then the number applies to each atom inside the parentheses. For example, the formula unit for the ionic compound calcium hydroxide, $Ca(OH)_2$, contains one calcium atom, two oxygen atoms, and two hydrogen atoms. The formula unit for aluminum sulfate, $Al_2(SO_4)_3$, contains two aluminum atoms, three sulfur atoms, and twelve oxygen atoms.

The **oxidation number** of an element indicates how many electrons an element is likely to gain, lose, or share in order to achieve an octet in its outer electron level when it bonds with other atoms. Therefore, the oxidation number of an element is directly related to the number of valence electrons it has.

Elements that have low electronegativities tend to have few valence electrons, and they lose electrons when they bond. These are assigned positive oxidation numbers. The alkali metals (Group IA) have only one valence electron. When they form ionic bonds, they lose their one electron, so they are assigned an oxidation number of $+1$. The alkaline-earth metals (Group IIA) lose two electrons and so are assigned an oxidation number of $+2$.

Elements that have high electronegativities tend to have many valence electrons, and they gain electrons when they bond to form a stable octet. These are assigned negative oxidation numbers. The members of the halogen family (Group VIIA), with seven valence electrons, gain one electron when they bond and are assigned oxidation numbers of -1. The members of the oxygen family (Group VIA) gain two electrons and are assigned the oxidation number of -2.

Most of the transition metals and some nonmetals can have more than one oxidation state, depending on the compound. It is possible to form two or more different compounds from the same elements.

When elements combine to form ionic compounds, the number of electrons lost must equal the number gained within a formula unit. The sum of the oxidation numbers in a correctly written formula for both ionic and covalent compounds will always equal zero. We use oxidation numbers to help us determine the correct chemical formula.

In this course, when writing the oxidation number, the sign precedes the number. However, when indicating the charge on an ion, the sign follows the number. For example, calcium is assigned an oxidation number of $+2$, but the charge on a calcium ion would be written as $2+$.

Exercises

Carefully read the example. Write the chemical formulas for the problems below.

Example

Problem: Write the chemical formula for a compound of calcium and bromine.

Step 1: Determine the oxidation numbers of the elements involved.

One Ca atom (Group IIA) has _____ valence electrons. When it bonds, Ca will _____ (gain/lose) _____ electron(s), resulting in a charge of _____. The oxidation number of Ca is _____.

One Br atom (Group VIIA) has _____ valence electrons. When it bonds, Br will _____ (gain/lose) _____ electron(s), resulting in a charge of _____. The oxidation number of Br is _____.

Step 2: Write the symbols of the two elements next to each other with the oxidation numbers of the elements above their symbols.

$$\overset{+2}{\textbf{Ca}} \quad \overset{-1}{\textbf{Br}}$$

Is the sum of the oxidation numbers zero? If not, you know that CaBr is not the correct formula.

Step 3: Determine which charge needs to increase in order to balance the formula. In this case, the negative charges need to increase. Add another bromine atom.

$$\overset{+2}{\textbf{Ca}} \quad \overset{2(-1)}{\textbf{Br}_2}$$

$(+2) + 2(-1) = 0$. The sum of the oxidation numbers is now zero; therefore, the formula $CaBr_2$ is correct.

Step 4: Write the correct formula: **CaBr₂**. Notice that the oxidation numbers are *not* part of the final formula.

When writing formulas involving elements with oxidation numbers that are not integer multiples of each other (for example, 2 and 3), use the *least common multiple* method as explained in your textbook.

A. Write the correct chemical formula for a compound that contains the following elements or ions. The applicable oxidation numbers are given in parentheses.

1. Li (+1)   and   Cl (−1)   _____

2. Na (+1)   and   Cl (−1)   _____

3. H (+1)   and   O (−2)   _____

4. Na (+1)   and OH^- (−1)   _____

5. Ca (+2)   and   O (−2)   _____

6. C (+4)   and   O (−2)   _____

7. S (+6)   and   O (−2)   _____

B. Whenever a chemical formula requires more than one polyatomic ion, parentheses must be included around the formula for the entire ion and the subscript should follow the parentheses.

Example   Mg (+2) and OH^- (−1) : **Mg(OH)₂**

1. Ba (+2)   and OH^- (−1)   : _____

2. Al (+3)   and OH^- (−1)   : _____

3. NH_4^+ (+1)   and   S (−2)   : _____

4. Al (+3)   and SO_4^{2-} (−2)   : _____

C. Apply What You Have Learned

1. The oxidation number of Mg is _____ and the oxidation number for Cl is _____. This means that each atom of Mg _____ (gains/loses) _____ electron(s) and each atom of Cl _____ (gains/loses) _____ electron(s). In the compound magnesium chloride, one atom of Mg will combine with _____ Cl atom(s) and the chemical formula is _____.

2. $Ca(OH)_2$ contains _____ atom(s) of calcium, _____ atom(s) of oxygen, and _____ atom(s) of hydrogen.

3. $Ca_3(PO_4)_2$ contains _____ atom(s) of calcium, _____ atom(s) of phosphorus, and _____ atom(s) of oxygen.

4. Oxygen almost always has an oxidation number of -2. Therefore, in the formula for magnetite, FeO, the oxidation number for iron must be _____. In the formula for rust, Fe_2O_3, the oxidation number for iron must be _____.

5. Based on the common oxidation number for chlorine, which is usually -1, the oxidation number for lead in $PbCl_2$ must be _____. In the compound lead oxide, PbO_2, the oxidation number for lead must be _____.

6. (Optional) As you can see, some metals can have more than one oxidation number. Write a brief rule that will allow you to determine the correct oxidation number of a metal in any given compound. _____

_____

_____

_____

Name _____

Date _____ Hour _____

Objectives

The purpose of this assignment is to

1. Review writing correct compound formulas and names.

2. Practice writing and balancing chemical equations.

Review Exercises

A. Writing Formulas

1. Write the compound formulas for the following combinations of elements and ions.

   a. C $(+4)$ and Cl (-1) → _____

   b. Ca $(+2)$ and OH^- (-1) → _____

   c. Al $(+3)$ and O (-2) → _____

2. $Ba(HCO_3)_2$ contains _____ atom(s) of barium, _____ atom(s) of hydrogen, _____ atom(s) of carbon, and _____ atom(s) of oxygen.

3. Use numbers to complete each of the following statements. Elements combine in specific ratios for each compound. Barium and chlorine will always react so that _____ atom(s) of Ba combine(s) with _____ atom(s) of Cl to form barium chloride. Therefore, the ratio of barium to chlorine is _____ : _____. If a sample of barium chloride contains 10 atoms of barium, it will have _____ atoms of chlorine. If a sample of barium chloride contains 1,000 atoms of chlorine, it will have _____ atoms of Ba.

B. Naming Compounds

Name the following compounds.

1. Na_2S _____

2. CO _____

3. NH_4Cl _____

4. Na_2CO_3 _____

5. CS_2 _____

6. $Mg(OH)_2$ _____

7. P_2O_5 _____

8. $Al_2(SO_4)_3$ _____

The same two elements can often form more than one ionic compound when the metal has more than one common oxidation number. Compounds of iron and oxygen are good examples of this. These elements can form both FeO and Fe_2O_3. If you called them both iron oxide, you could not tell them apart. Chemists use a notation called the *Stock system* to differentiate between them. The Stock system inserts a Roman numeral in parentheses after the metal in the compound name. The Roman numeral is equal to the oxidation number of the metal. The iron and oxygen compounds mentioned are then named iron(II) oxide and iron(III) oxide, respectively. **Note that the Stock system is not used for metals that have only one common oxidation number and never for naming covalent compounds.**

Practice naming the following compounds using the Stock system:

9. FeS   _____

10. $Pb(NO_3)_2$ _____

11. Cu_2SO_4 _____

Balancing Equations

Write and balance the formula equations for the following word equations. Refer to your textbook, p. 199, to review the steps to follow. If either a reactant or a product occurs as a diatomic molecule, be sure to write its formula correctly. The first problem is done as an example.

1. Silver nitrate plus copper metal produces copper(II) nitrate plus silver metal.

    Write: $AgNO_3 + Cu \rightarrow Cu(NO_3)_2 + Ag$

    a. It is often best to begin with the most complicated formula first—in this case, $Cu(NO_3)_2$. Notice that there are two nitrate groups on the right, so a 2 must be written in front of the $AgNO_3$.

    $$2\, AgNO_3 + Cu \rightarrow Cu(NO_3)_2 + Ag$$

    b. Now there are two Ag on the left, so you must write a 2 in front of Ag on the right. (Pure metals are never given subscripts when balancing equations.)

    c. There is one Cu on the left and there is one on the right, so they are balanced.

    d. The balanced equation is $2AgNO_3 + Cu \rightarrow Cu(NO_3)_2 + 2Ag$.

2. Barium plus water produces barium hydroxide and hydrogen gas.

3. Aluminum plus fluorine produces aluminum fluoride.

4. Mercury (II) oxide is decomposed with heat to form metallic mercury and gaseous oxygen.

5. Supply the missing coefficients and symbols to balance each equation.

    a. _____ H_2 + _____ → _____

    b. _____ Zn + _____ $AgNO_3$ → _____ $Zn(NO_3)_2$ + _____

Chemical Reactions

Name _____

Date _____ Hour _____

Objectives

The purpose of this demonstration is to

1. Observe four types of chemical reactions.

2. Determine the type of reaction when given the chemical equation.

Materials

Copper sulfate solution
Powdered zinc

Equipment

Apron
Beakers (50 mL), 3
Bunsen burner
Bunsen burner lighter
Chemical scoop
Crucible tongs
Graduated cylinder, 25 mL
Stirring rod
Tripod
Wire gauze square

Introduction

Scientists are able to classify most chemical reactions into four general types. **Combination reactions** (also called synthesis reactions) combine two or more substances to form one product. They take the form

$$X + Y \rightarrow XY$$

The reactants can be elements or compounds, solid, liquid, or gas, but the key feature of this type of reaction is that there is more than one reactant but only one product.

Examples: $2Na + Cl_2 \rightarrow 2NaCl$

$H_2O + SO_3 \rightarrow H_2SO_4$

In **decomposition reactions,** one reactant breaks apart to form two or more products. The form of this reaction is

$$XY \rightarrow X + Y$$

Heat or electrical energy is usually required to decompose substances. The key feature of this type of reaction is that there is only one reactant, but there are several products. Many decomposition reactions give off a gas as a product.

Example: $CaCO_3 \rightarrow CaO + CO_2$

In a **single-replacement reaction,** one more active element takes the place of a less active element in a compound. The form of this reaction is

$$X + YZ \rightarrow XZ + Y$$

X and *Y* are (usually) metal elements and *Z* may be either an element or a polyatomic anion. The activity of an element is generally related to its electronegativity. The more electronegative metal will usually be replaced by the less electronegative one. It is this difference in bond energy that causes the reaction to take place. In order to predict whether one element will replace another in a compound, you need to know the relative electronegativities of the different elements. This information is found in many chemistry textbooks.

Examples: $Mg + 2HCl \rightarrow MgCl_2 + H_2$

$Zn + H_2SO_4 \rightarrow ZnSO_4 + H_2$

A **double-replacement reaction** almost always involves a combination of two ionic solutions. The form of this reaction is

$$WX + YZ \rightarrow WZ + YX$$

There are always two reactants and two products. It is called a double-replacement because both cations and both anions take the opposite partners. Because the ions are dissociated, or separated from each other in solution, the ions are free to combine in new ways. This type of reaction often results in a solid precipitating out of the solution, the formation of a gas, or the production of water, which becomes part of the water in the solution.

Example: $NaCl + AgNO_3 \rightarrow NaNO_3 + AgCl$*(ppt)*

Pre-Laboratory Questions

Read the entire investigation. Answer the following questions prior to class on a separate sheet of paper. Use complete sentences.

1. What products do you expect to result from the electrolysis of water?

2. What can be done to make the electrolysis of pure water more efficient?

3. Name the reactants in this investigation that, when combined, will most likely form a precipitate.

4. Which type of reaction almost always involves two ionic compounds?

5. If there is not enough of a reactant to completely combine with another reactant, what do we call the first reactant?

6. Which type of reaction always yields only a single product?

7. How is the reaction between zinc and sulfur started?

8. What color does the copper(II) ion (Cu^{2+}) impart to a solution?

9. Why is the copper(II) sulfate solution heated before it is added to the zinc?

Procedures

A. Electrolysis of Water

Water is composed of the two elements oxygen and hydrogen. When an electric current is passed through water, the electrical energy breaks the chemical bonds holding the oxygen and hydrogen together. Oxygen (O_2) is formed at the positive electrode, and hydrogen (H_2) is formed at the negative one. This process is called electrolysis. Often an ionic solute such as potassium hydroxide (KOH) is added to the pure water to improve the process.

Write a balanced chemical equation for the electrolysis of water. _____

_____

Examine the form of this equation and state what type of reaction it is. _____

_____

1. Observe as your teacher operates the electrolysis apparatus. What do you notice accumulating in the inverted test tubes? _____

_____

2. Why would you want to include an ionic solute in the electrolysis solution?

_____

_____

3. Look at the product side of the electrolysis reaction. How should the volume of hydrogen produced compare to the volume of oxygen? Why?

_____

_____

B. Lead nitrate ($Pb(NO_3)_2$) and potassium chromate (K_2CrO_4)

What happens when a solution of potassium chromate is added to a solution of lead nitrate? Before these two ionic solutions are mixed together, all of the ions are dissociated. When they are mixed, however, the lead ions (Pb^{2+}) form bonds with the chromate ions (CrO_4^{2-}), forming a solid that separates out of the solution (a precipitate) and leaving the potassium (K^+) and nitrate (NO_3^-) ions still dissociated in the solution. If you do not add enough chromate ions to pair up with all of the lead ions, there will still be lead ions in the solution when the reaction is finished. When there is not enough of one reactant to completely combine with the other reactant, the first is called the *limiting reactant*. If you had an abundance of chromate ions and fewer lead ions, the lead would be the limiting reactant.

Write a balanced chemical equation for the reaction. _____

_____

Examine the form of the equation and state what type of reaction this is. _____

_____

1. Your teacher will first put an eyedropper full of lead nitrate in a test tube.

2. Observe as your teacher adds drop by drop an eyedropper full of potassium chromate solution to the test tube that contains the lead nitrate solution.

3. What evidence do you observe that a chemical reaction has taken place?

_____

4. What is the chemical formula of the precipitate? _____

5. What is the chemical formula of the compound that remained in solution in the test tube? _____

6. Lead chromate was an ingredient in exterior and interior house paint for many years. Why do you think that commercially available house paint no longer contains lead-based compounds? _____

_____

_____

7. (Optional) How did your teacher separate the lead chromate from the dissolved compound? _____

_____

C. Zinc and Sulfur

Zinc (Zn) is assigned an oxidation number of +2 because it has two valence electrons. Sulfur (S), being a member of the oxygen family, is assigned an oxidation number of −2. When ignited, these two elements will react to form a new compound, zinc sulfide.

Write a balanced chemical equation for this reaction. _____

Examine the form of the equation and state what type of reaction this is. _____

_____

1. Enter the chemical formula of the product of the reaction in the data table below.

2. Note the appearance of the zinc and the sulfur as demonstrated to you by your teacher. Record your observations in the table.

3. Watch as your teacher mixes the zinc and the sulfur and ignites it. Do not look directly at the magnesium strip as it is burning.

4. What evidence did you observe that a chemical reaction has taken place?

_____

5. Record the appearance of the product of the reaction in the data table.

6. If this reaction forms only one product, what substance is in the smoke?

_____

Data Table: Zinc and Sulfur

	Appearance
Sulfur (S)	
Zinc (Zn)	
Product _____	

D. Zinc and Copper Sulfate

Your teacher may have you perform this demonstration yourself. If so, carefully follow the instructions below. What happens when you add metallic zinc (Zn) to a solution of copper sulfate ($CuSO_4$)? Because the zinc is a more "active" metal, it will take the place of the copper, leaving the copper as a metal solid in the resulting zinc sulfate solution. The blue color of copper sulfate solutions is due to the presence of the copper(II) ion (Cu^{2+}). If you added enough zinc, the solution would appear colorless because the zinc would completely replace the copper ions in solution.

Write a balanced chemical equation for the reaction (assume an oxidation state of +2 for the Zn). _____

Examine the form of the equation and state what type of reaction this is. _____

_____

1. Label three 50 mL beakers **1, 2,** and **3.** Add 18 mL of $CuSO_4$ solution to both beakers **1** and **2.**

2. Measure about 0.9 g of powdered zinc with a balance. Add the zinc to beaker **3.**

3. Place beaker **1** on the wire gauze on the tripod. Light the Bunsen burner and warm the solution gently. Do not cause the solution to boil.

4. Turn off the Bunsen burner. Using crucible tongs, remove beaker **1** from the tripod and slowly pour the warm $CuSO_4$ onto the powdered zinc in beaker **3.** Stir the reactants with a stirring rod during the addition. If the reactants begin to froth, pour more slowly.

5. When the reaction has ceased, place beakers **2** and **3** side by side.

6. What color is the solution in beaker **2?** _____

7. What is the appearance and color of the solid in beaker **3?** _____

   _____

8. List the observations that indicate to you that a chemical reaction has taken place in the experimental beaker. _____

   _____

   _____

9. In this reaction, what happened to the copper and the zinc? _____

   _____

   _____

10. Which beaker was the experimental control? _____

   _____

10 INVESTIGATION
Phase Changes in Solutions

Name _____

Date_____ Hour_____

Objective

The purpose of this investigation is to demonstrate the effect of a solute on the freezing and boiling points of water.

Materials

Distilled water
Ice
Table salt

Equipment

Beakers (250 mL), 2
Beakers (500 mL), 3
Beaker tongs
Bunsen burner
Burner lighter
Stirring rods, 2
Tablespoon
Thermometers, 2
Tripod
Wire gauze

Introduction

We know from observing the various substances that make up our physical environment that different substances have different freezing and boiling points. Pure water freezes at 0.0°C and boils at 100.0°C. Pure acetic acid, however, which is also a liquid at room temperature, freezes at 16.6°C and boils at 117.9°C. The melting and boiling points for each substance are different because the strengths of the forces between particles varies with the substance. For example, the particles (ions) of ionic solids are held together by extremely strong electrostatic forces. As a result, ionic compounds generally have much higher melting points than do covalent compounds, whose molecules are held together by relatively weak intermolecular forces.

Boiling points of liquids are affected by atmospheric pressure as well as bond strength. The values given above for the boiling points of water and acetic acid are the values determined at one atmosphere of air pressure (measured at sea level). If you were to climb a mountain to an altitude of one mile and compare boiling point temperatures, you would find them somewhat lower than normal because of the decrease in the air pressure. Since water boils at a lower temperature at higher altitudes, food must be cooked for a longer time. This is why you may see alternate cooking directions for higher elevations included on the containers of many prepackaged foods.

A **solution,** you will recall from your textbook, is a type of homogeneous mixture in which a **solute** is dissolved in a **solvent.** The question for this investigation is "Will the presence of a solute affect the phase changes of a solution?" It has been found that solutions do not freeze or boil at the same temperature as the pure solvent. Why is this? Let's start with pure water as an example. Water molecules have a certain attraction for each other. At temperatures just above the freezing point, the attractive forces and the disruptive effects of molecular motion are balanced. The molecules are still vibrating too fast to be held in the solid crystal form (ice). As the water molecules lose kinetic energy (cool down), the attractive forces of the molecules for each other become strong enough to pull them into the ice crystal structure and the water freezes. Adding a solute, however, interferes with the freezing process by physically getting in the way of the water molecules lining up with each other to form the crystal structure. The water molecules thus need to lose even more kinetic energy (get even cooler than usual) in order to freeze. For this reason, pure seawater that is 3.5 percent salt by mass freezes at around −1.2°C. With few exceptions, adding any solute to any solvent causes a lowering of the freezing point, or **freezing point depression.**

Solutes also tend to interfere with the boiling process. At the normal boiling point, water molecules only have to break away from the attraction of other water molecules. But the presence of solute particles increases the attractive forces on individual water molecules, so they need greater kinetic energy to break free. This translates into a higher boiling temperature. Pure seawater boils at about 100.3°C. This increase in boiling point is called **boiling point elevation.** The magnitude of these two effects (called *colligative effects*) depends on the solvent (*not* the solute) and the concentration of the solute.

Pre-Laboratory Questions

Read the entire investigation. Answer the following questions prior to class on a separate sheet of paper. Use complete sentences.

1. For salt water, state which is the solute and which is the solvent.

2. What effect does a solute have on the boiling and freezing points of a solvent?

3. In the section of the investigation measuring boiling point elevation, which beaker is the control? Why is it important to include this?

4. Why should you *not* stir the ice slurry with a thermometer?

5. State the research question.

6. State your hypothesis regarding the relationship between presence of a solute and solvent phase changes.

Procedures

A. Boiling Point Elevation

1. Using masking tape, label one thermometer "beaker 1" and the other "beaker 2." Use these thermometers only in their respective beakers for the entire investigation.

2. Label two 250 mL beakers "1" and "2" with a water-soluble marker. Pour about 150 mL of distilled water into each beaker.

3. Add about 15 cm^3 (one tablespoon) of NaCl to the water in beaker 2 and stir until the salt is completely dissolved.

4. Place beaker 1 on top of the wire gauze on the tripod.

5. Light the Bunsen burner and heat the water to a rolling boil.

6. Measure the temperature of the beaker **while the water is boiling.** Make sure the thermometer is submerged in the water without touching either the sides or the bottom of the beaker. Keep the thermometer in the water until the temperature no longer changes.

7. Record the boiling temperature for distilled water in the data table. Report temperature to the nearest 0.1°C.

8. Using the beaker tongs, carefully remove the beaker from the tripod and pour the hot water in the sink.

9. Repeat Steps 3–7 with beaker 2 containing the salt water.

10. Turn off the Bunsen burner.

11. Wash and dry both beakers.

12. Obtain distilled and salt water boiling point data from three other groups and record them in the data table.

13. Average the observed boiling points for the distilled and saltwater samples and record these temperatures in Table 1 (to the nearest 0.1°C).

B. Freezing Point Depression

1. Label two 500 mL beakers "1" and "2." Fill each of them to the rim with cold, crushed ice.

2. In a third 500 mL beaker or other clean container, mix 300 mL of distilled water and 30 cm^3 (2 tablespoons) of salt until the salt is completely dissolved.

3. Pour 300 mL of distilled water over the ice in beaker 1 and the salt solution over the ice in beaker 2.

4. Stir both beakers with a separate stirring rod continuously. Observe the temperature of the ice slurry in each beaker every 60 seconds and note the temperature on a piece of scratch paper. **Do not stir with the thermometers!**

5. When the temperature of the slurry has not changed for two measurements, or if you note the temperature beginning to rise, record the lowest temperature observed in Table 2. Report temperature to the nearest 0.1°C.

6. Pour the ice water slurries into the sink. Wash and dry both beakers, utensils, and the thermometers.

7. Obtain distilled and salt water temperature data from the same three groups as in part A above and record them in the data table.

8. Average the lowest recorded temperature for the distilled and salt water and record this value in the data table (to the nearest 0.1°C.)

Results

Table 1: Boiling Points of Water Solutions

	Distilled	Salt
(Your group)		
Group _____		
Group _____		
Group _____		
Averages—		

Table 2: Freezing Points of Water Solutions

	Distilled	Salt
(Your group)		
Group _____		
Group _____		
Group _____		
Averages—		

Discussion

1. Summarize the observations made in this investigation. _____

   _____

   _____

2. From a molecular point of view, make a general inference from these observations. In other words, why did the boiling and freezing points change? _____

   _____

3. Would your interpretation of the facts be different if you had not included the controls in this experiment? _____

   _____

   _____

4. Based on this investigation, why do you think salt is added to the ice surrounding the freezer when making homemade ice cream? _____

   _____

   _____

5. Why is salt sometimes spread on icy roads? _____

   _____

   _____

6. What do you think would have happened to the boiling point of the water if you had added more salt? _____

   _____

Experimental Evaluation

7. What was the highest recorded temperature for distilled water *boiling point?* What was the lowest? What is the difference in these two temperatures? Show your calculations. _____

_____

_____

8. What is the difference between the average distilled water boiling point and 100.0°C? Show your calculations. _____

_____

_____

_____

9. What is the difference between the salt water average boiling point and the distilled water average boiling point? Show your calculations. _____

_____

_____

10. How do instrumental errors affect the measuring of physical quantities? How are the effects of these errors minimized when collecting data?

_____

_____

_____

_____

11. What other factor could have influenced boiling point measurements? (Review the Introduction.) _____

_____

_____

_____

Name _____

Date _____ Hour _____

Objectives

The purpose of this exercise is to

1. Observe the use of various pH indicators and methods.

2. Determine the pH of several common substances.

Materials

Ammonia, household
Clear soda
Cola
Dishwashing detergent
HCl solution
Lemon juice
Litmus paper
Milk
NaOH solution
pHydrion™ paper or equivalent
Vinegar
Other household items (optional)
Bromothymol blue indicator (optional)
Phenolphthalein indicator (optional)

Equipment

Beakers, 50 mL
Eyedroppers
Test tubes
Test tube racks

Introduction

The pH of solutions can be determined subjectively by acid-base indicators. Recall from your textbook that these are organic substances that change color in the presence of an acid or a base. Litmus is an indicator extracted from a certain kind of lichen, a mossy substance that grows on rocks and trees. In its indicator form, litmus is red from a pH of 0.0 to 4.5 (acid) and blue from 8.3 to 14.0 (base). Between a pH of 4.5 and 8.3, the color of the chemical is intermediate between red and blue and is not a good indicator of the pH. Litmus is used to determine if a substance is an acid or a base, but it cannot provide numerical pH values. Other pH indicators, such as phenolphthalein or bromothymol blue, change color at different, specific pH values. They can tell you whether the pH is above or below their specific turning points, but, like litmus, they cannot give you a specific pH determination. Some substances turn many colors over a wide range of pH values. These indicators are the most useful because they can determine not only whether a solution is an acid or a base, but they can also indicate the numerical pH of the solution. This kind of substance is called a **universal indicator**. pHydrion paper is one such indicator. The numerical pH value of the tested solution is determined by comparing the color of the universal indicator in the solution with a standardized color chart that is provided by the manufacturer.

Pre-Laboratory Questions

Read the entire investigation. Answer the following questions prior to class on a separate sheet of paper. Use complete sentences.

1. From what is the chemical litmus obtained? For what is it used?

2. Between what pH values is litmus not a reliable indicator?

3. What information can the indicator phenolphthalein give you?.

4. What specific information do universal indicators provide that many other indicators are not able to provide?

5. Why shouldn't you use the same eyedropper for several chemicals when transferring chemicals from one container to another?

Procedures

Testing stations are placed around the room with various pH indicators and substances. Carefully read and follow the instructions below. The results from the stations testing the specific indicators will be entered in Table 2. When testing pH using any kind of testing paper, dispose of the paper in the container provided. When using eyedroppers, use only the eyedropper labeled for its solution. When finished with the eyedropper, return any unused chemical to the proper container and lay it down on the paper towel provided. Promptly wipe up any spills.

A. Stations A - ____, Testing Common Solutions for pH

Your teacher will have several stations set up to test the pH of some common solutions. You will be using the universal indicator paper at each station to obtain a numerical value for the pH. Follow the steps below.

1. Dip a piece of the universal indicator paper into the solution.

2. Match the resulting color to the color scale on the indicator-paper package.

3. Record the numerical pH and whether the solution is an acid or a base in Table 1 below.

4. Dispose of the paper in the container provided.

B. Litmus Paper Station

Correct Use of Litmus Paper

1. Dip one piece each of blue and red (pink) litmus paper in distilled water. What happens? _____

2. Dip a piece of blue litmus paper into the NaOH solution. What happens?

   _____

3. Dip a piece of red (pink) litmus paper into the NaOH solution. What happens? _____ The color change indicates that NaOH in water is a(n) _____.

4. Enter the color the litmus turned in NaOH in Row 1 of Table 2 under the column for base color.

5. Which step, 1 or 2, served as the control? Why? _____

_____

Incorrect Use

6. Dip a fresh piece of red litmus paper in the NaOH solution. What happens?

_____

7. After blotting the blue end of the same litmus paper on a paper towel, dip it into the HCl solution. What happens? _____

_____

8. After blotting the wet end of the same litmus paper on a paper towel, again dip it into the NaOH solution. What happens? _____

_____

9. What would happen if you did not blot the excess chemical before testing the other solution? _____

_____

10. How do you prevent this kind of problem from occurring when testing several solutions in a row? _____

_____

C. Red Cabbage Extract Station

1. Add one dropper full of ammonia to one test tube. Add one dropper full of HCl to another test tube.

2. Test each of the solutions with the universal indicator paper. Match the resulting color to the color scale on the indicator-paper package. Record the pH values in Table 2 for red cabbage extract.

3. Add one dropper full of the cabbage extract to the two test tubes.

4. Note the color in each solution and record your results in Table 2.

5. Based on your observations, for what kind of scientific purpose could you use red cabbage extract? _____

_____

6. Rinse the test tubes with water and place them upside down in the test tube rack.

D. Bromothymol Blue Station (Optional)

1. Add one dropper full of NaOH solution to one test tube and a dropper full of HCl solution to a second test tube.

2. Add two drops of bromothymol blue indicator to each of the test tubes.

3. Record the resulting colors in Table 2.

4. Rinse the tubes with water and place them upside down in the test tube rack.

E. Phenolphthalein Station (Optional)

1. Add one dropper full of NaOH solution to one test tube and a dropper full of HCl solution to a second test tube.

2. Place two drops of phenolphthalein indicator into each of the test tubes.

3. Record the resulting colors in Table 2.

4. Rinse the tubes with water and place them upside down in the test tube rack.

Results

Table 1: pH of Common Solutions

Station	Solution	pH	Acid or Base?	Station	Solution	pH	Acid or Base?
A				I			
B				J			
C				K			
D				L			
E				M			
F				N			
G				O			
H				P			

Table 2: Indicator Color Ranges

Indicator	Acid		Base	
	Color	pH (Range)	Color	pH (Range)
Litmus				
Red Cabbage Extract				
Bromothymol Blue				
Phenolphthalein				

Note: You can obtain pH range information from science supply catalogs, *The Merck Manual,* or on the Internet.

Discussion Questions

1. What was the most basic solution tested? Most acidic? _____

   _____

   _____

2. Bases produce an excess of _____ ions.

3. Acids produce an excess of _____ ions.

4. At a pH of 7, the concentrations of H_3O^+ and OH^- ions are [different] [equal] (circle one).

5. The numbers on the pH scale go from _____ to _____.

6. The numbers for the pH scale indicate the concentration of what ions?

_____

7. Substances that are acidic taste [sour] [bitter]. Farmers in times past have tasted the soil to determine its quality. If the soil tasted slightly sour, they would say that the soil needed to be sweetened. This was usually done by adding ashes or, today, by adding lime. This simple taste test indicated that the soil needed to be made more [acidic] [basic].

8. It can be observed that many preferred food items tend to be [acidic] [basic] and cleaning items tend to be [acidic] [basic].

Experimental Evaluation

9. The acid-base indicators used in this investigation gave pH values to the nearest [ones] [tenths] [hundredths] place.

10. Work with DNA often requires pH values to the nearest tenths place. Would any of the tests in this investigation be suitable? Explain. _____

_____

11. In what pH range would litmus paper give an uncertain result? _____

_____

12. Can litmus paper be used to test the pH of water (pure or tap)? Explain.

_____

_____

13. What serves as the control (basis of comparison) for the universal pH paper? _____

12 APPLICATIONS
Stopping Distances

Name _____

Date_____ Hour_____

Objective

The purpose of this exercise is to show the relationships among the speed of a car, its kinetic energy, and the distance it takes to stop.

Introduction

Mathematical formulas are equations that relate two or more measurable physical quantities to each other. Because they are equations, it is never appropriate to give only one side or the other of the formula. For example, if you were asked for the formula for kinetic energy, you should provide $K.E. = \frac{1}{2}mv^2$, not just $\frac{1}{2}mv^2$. Formulas are essential for understanding how the physical world works. They represent the orderliness of physical processes. When studying mechanical motion, it is often easier to assume that motion is in geometrically simple patterns such as straight lines, and we ignore effects such as friction, which are not important at this time. This allows the formulas we use to be as simple as possible so that we can better understand the underlying principles. Of course, the result often does not exactly match what is seen in the real world.

In Chapter 12, you learned about the conservation of energy and the transformation of one form of energy into another. In particular, you learned about mechanical energy and momentum. In this exercise, you are going to gain an appreciation for the mechanical energy contained in a moving car—something that will be very valuable to know as you begin to learn about driving. As mentioned in the paragraph above, we will be making some simplifying assumptions to help us understand the problems and the principles involved.

Assumptions:

1. The car is traveling in a straight line.

2. All conditions are normal and optimal—alert, skilled driver; dry, clean road pavement; brakes work continuously at maximum efficiency until the car stops.

3. The car slows at a constant -5.0 m/s^2 when the brakes are applied under the above conditions.

Recall that a negative acceleration means that the car is reducing its speed with time. The assumptions are reasonable and realistic except for idealized brake operation and constant deceleration. These are allowed so that you can make some calculations using math you are familiar with.

Problems

Solve the following problems according to the directions for each. Show your work in the space provided below each question. Write your final answers in the specified table. Include the correct units. If you are observing significant digits (SDs), round your final answer to the correct number of SDs; otherwise, round your answers to one decimal place.

Stopping Distances

Definitions

d is the distance traveled in an interval of time. Units are kilometers, meters, centimeters, and so on. Its formula is $d = r \cdot t$. The rate, r, is the same as average velocity, v_{avg}.

t is the length of the time interval. Units are hours, minutes, or seconds.

v is the speed of an object. Units are in km/h, m/s, and so on.

v_{avg} is the average speed during an interval of time. Its formula is

$$v_{avg} = \frac{v_1 + v_2}{2}.$$

m is the mass of an object. Units are kilograms, grams, and so on.

a is the acceleration of an object, the change in speed in a given time interval. Its formula is $a = \dfrac{v_2 - v_1}{t}$.

Subscript 1 refers to the first measurement taken during a time interval.

Subscript 2 refers to the second or last measurement taken during a time interval.

Stopping Distance

Suppose a car is moving 5.0 m/s (11 mph). How far will it take the car to stop if it can decelerate at -5.0 m/s^2?

1. The given information is the initial speed ($v_1 = 5.0$ m/s) and the acceleration ($a = -5.0$ m/s^2). We are looking for the distance (d) traveled until the car stops ($v_2 = 0.0$ m/s).

2. To find distance, we see that the applicable formula is $d = v_{avg} \cdot t$.

3. The car slows from 5.0 m/s to 0.0 m/s; therefore, the average velocity will be

_____

4. In order to find the distance, you must still find elapsed time. The only formula provided that has all of the required information is that for acceleration: $a = \dfrac{v_2 - v_1}{t}$.

   $a = $ _____

   $v_1 = $ _____

   $v_2 = $ _____

Rearrange the acceleration formula and solve for t before substituting values.

$t =$ _____ (Rearrange)

$t =$ _____ (Substitute)

$t =$ _____ (Solve) Write this answer in Table 1 for "Time" at 5.0 m/s.

5. Now the original distance equation (see 2, above) can be solved.

$d =$ _____ (Substitute)

$d =$ _____ (Solve) Write this answer in Table 1 for "Distance" at 5.0 m/s.

6. Using the same process, fill in Table 1 for 10. m/s and 20. m/s. Show your work in the spaces below (remember that a decimal point after a trailing zero indicates that the zero is significant).

$v_1 = 10.$ m/s, $a = -5.0$ m/s^2 $v_1 = 20.$ m/s, $a = -5.0$ m/s^2

_____   _____

_____   _____

_____   _____

Table 1: Stopping Distances

Velocity	Time	Distance in m and ft.
5.0 m/s (11 mph)		
10. m/s (22 mph)		
20. m/s (45 mph)		

Kinetic Energy of the Car (Collision Energy)

Suppose the car has a mass of 1000. kg (2200 lb.). How much kinetic energy will the car have at a speed of 5.0 m/s?

1. The kinetic energy formula is K.E. $= \frac{1}{2} mv^2$.

$m = $ _____ $v = $ _____

$K.E. = $ _____   (Substitute)

$K.E. = $ _____   (Solve) Record this answer for a velocity of 5.0 m/s in Table 2, below.

2. Calculate the kinetic energies for the same car at 10. m/s and 20. m/s and enter them in Table 2.

$m = $ _____ $v = $ _____ $m = $ _____ $v = $ _____

$K.E. = $ _____ $K.E. = $ _____

$K.E. = $ _____ $K.E. = $ _____

Table 2: Kinetic Energies

Velocity	Kinetic Energy
5.0 m/s	
10. m/s	
20. m/s	

Discussion Questions

1. If the initial speed of the car is doubled, its new stopping distance will be about _____ times its original stopping distance.

2. If the initial speed of the car is doubled, its new kinetic energy will be about _____ times its original kinetic energy.

3. If a safe distance behind another car driving 30 mph is 40 feet (12 m), you should stay _____ behind a car on the highway when driving 60 mph.

4. A collision at 60 mph will be _____ times more energetic than a collision at 30 mph.

5. In your own words give two important driving principles illustrated by this study. _____

_____

_____

Experimental Evaluation

6. In order to solve these problems, certain assumptions were made. List these assumptions. _____

_____

_____

_____

_____

_____

7. List some of the factors discussed in the Facet on page 276 of your textbook that make one or more of these assumptions invalid in the real world. _____

_____

_____

_____

8. (Optional) Discuss why a safe following distance may be less than the braking distance for a given speed (see page 276 in your textbook).

_____

_____

_____

_____

_____

9. (Optional) In question 4 above, what were some assumptions that you made to answer the question? _____

_____

_____

_____

10. (Optional) In a collision of your car with another, what are some other factors besides the speed of your car that would determine the severity of the accident?

_____

_____

_____

13A APPLICATIONS

Yellow Light: Stop or Go?

Objectives

The purpose of this problem-solving exercise is to

1. Use basic equations of motion to investigate what can happen when a speeding car approaches a yellow light.

2. Determine some dynamic effects on the vehicle in this situation.

Introduction

You are driving a brand new SUV, approaching an intersection controlled by traffic lights. In your lane the light is green. Just seconds from the intersection, though, the light turns yellow. What are you going to do? In a split second you must decide whether there is enough time to go through the light while it is still yellow and, at the same time, estimate if you have enough room to stop safely if you want to stop. This is a real-world situation that drivers face all of the time.

We are going to apply some of the principles you have learned in Chapter 13 to this question. Scientific investigations often require simplified mathematical models in order to understand the complicated underlying principles. Scientists develop mathematical models to study problems that are too small, too large, or too complex to observe directly. Often the problem is simplified by making certain assumptions as we did in Applications 12 when studying stopping distances. This exercise will take this approach and then draw some inferences to real driving conditions.

In our problem, should you increase speed, coast, or try to stop? Your decision should be based on the following considerations: the approaching speed of the vehicle, the distance to the stoplight, the time duration until the traffic light turns red, the working condition of the brakes, your experience, and the road conditions. Traffic engineers take all of these factors into consideration and have coordinated safe speed limits with the duration of the yellow traffic light for normal driving conditions. This exercise will investigate some of the effects on a vehicle only when it coasts or tries to stop as it approaches a yellow traffic light. The option of increasing the car's speed to make it through the light will not be considered since this is unwise as well as illegal in most states.

Problems

Assumptions

1. No part of your vehicle is allowed to be in the intersection when the light turns red.

2. "In the intersection" means within the street area between the near curb and the far curb.

3. The street is 10. m (33 ft.) wide.

4. The SUV is 5.0 m (16.5 ft.) long.

5. You, the driver, are alert and skilled.

6. The road conditions are ideal.

7. The SUV's brakes are working properly.

8. You begin braking the same instant that the light turns yellow.

Initial Conditions

We will first consider the situation where you are approaching an intersection in a 30 mph zone. You are exceeding the speed limit, moving at 25 m/s (55 mph). The light turns yellow and it is timed to be on for 2.0 seconds before changing to red. Keeping in mind the assumptions, do you coast through the light at constant speed or do you brake to a stop (decelerate at -5.0 m/s^2 or -11 mph/s)?

Fill in the table with the initial conditions provided. These values can be considered realistic.

Initial Conditions

Condition	Value
Speed (m/s)	
Yellow Light Time (s)	
Deceleration (m/s^2)	

Coasting Through the Yellow Light

Assume you choose to coast through the yellow light—in other words, you will maintain constant speed. You believe that the combination of your speed and the remaining distance to the far side of the intersection will permit you to clear the intersection in 2.0 seconds or less. How far can you be from the intersection and coast through? This is the same as asking how far can the vehicle travel in 2.0 seconds. To answer this question, complete the following steps.

1. Picture the problem. Examine the diagram and write in the values of the initial conditions.

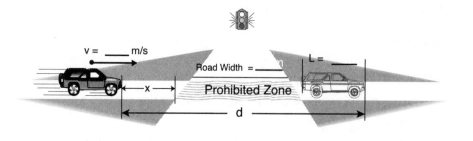

2. Write the applicable equation. _____

3. d = _____   (substitute)

4. d = _____   (solve)

5. What must you do to find the maximum distance to the intersection to safely coast through (x)? _____

_____

6. Calculate x: _____

7. At 55 mph, if you are **less than** _____ from the intersection, you can safely coast through the yellow light.

8. How many car lengths is this distance? _____

Recall that you were speeding in this situation!

9. Calculate in the space below the maximum distance that you could safely coast through the light if you were driving at the speed limit (13 m/s).

_____

_____

10. At 30 mph, if you are less than _____ from the intersection, you can safely coast through the yellow light. In car lengths, this distance is _____ car lengths.

Braking for the Yellow Light

Assume now that you decide to stop. You believe that there is sufficient distance for you to safely slow to a stop from the speed you are driving, considering the assumptions given. How far can you be from the intersection while driving 55 mph (25 m/s) and slowing to a stop by braking hard (-5.0 m/s²)? We will use the same distance equation as in the first case, but you are missing some information that will have to be found by additional calculations. Complete the following steps to find the answer.

1. Picture the problem. Examine the diagram and write in the values of the initial conditions.

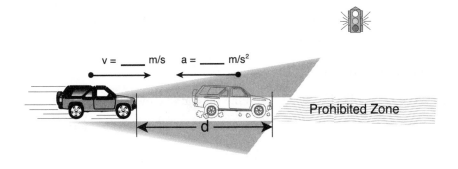

v = ____ m/s a = ____ m/s²   Prohibited Zone d

2. Write the applicable equation. _____

3. Since the speed is changing while the SUV is stopping, you will have to find its average speed, v_{avg}, to solve for d. To find v_{avg}, we must average the initial and final speeds. The initial speed (v_1) is _____, and the final speed (v_2) is _____.

v_{avg} = _____

4. Stopping time must be found using the acceleration formula $a =$ _____.

Rearranging: $t =$ _____

Solve for t: _____

5. We now have average speed and time. Calculate in the space below the minimum distance required to stop safely without entering the intersection.

_____

6. At 55 mph, if you are **more than** _____ from the intersection, you can safely stop for a yellow light.

7. How many car lengths is this distance? _____

8. Calculate in the space below the minimum distance required to safely stop for the light if you were driving at the speed limit (13 m/s).

v_{avg} =

t =

d =

9. At 30 mph, if you are **more than** _____ from the intersection, you can safely stop for the yellow light. In car lengths, this distance is _____ car lengths.

Evaluating the Results

1. Write the applicable distances in the diagram below:

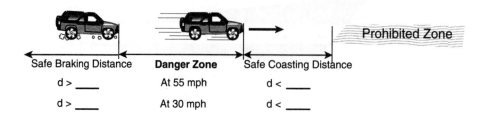

Safe Braking Distance	**Danger Zone**	Safe Coasting Distance
d > ____	At 55 mph	d < ____
d > ____	At 30 mph	d < ____

Chapter 13

2. Why is the space between the safe coasting distance and the safe braking distance called the "danger zone"? _____

_____

_____

3. If you believe you are in the danger zone as you approach a traffic light, what is your safest option? _____

_____

4. How would a traffic engineer eliminate the danger zone at this traffic light, assuming the speed limit must remain 30 mph? _____

_____

_____

5. Which assumption stated at the beginning of the exercise was the least realistic? _____

_____

6. What real-world effect would this have on the problem? _____

_____

_____

_____

_____

7. Based on what you have learned, give a reason that speeding is dangerous.

_____

_____

_____

Dynamics of Stopping a Vehicle

1. Assume that your SUV has a mass of 1500. kg. What force must be applied to the vehicle to stop it at the assumed deceleration of −5.0 m/s²? Recall that deceleration is negative acceleration.

   a. Write the formula that relates mass, acceleration, and force: _____

   _____

   b. Solve for force: $F =$ _____

   c. Why is this force negative? _____

   _____

   d. Where does this force come from to stop the vehicle? _____

   _____

   e. The force exerted by the brakes through the wheels contacts the ground. Which law of motion says that the ground will push back at the wheels with the same force but in the opposite direction? _____

   _____

   f. What physically happens to a vehicle when the ground cannot push back with the same reaction force as the vehicle exerts when it is slowing?

   _____

2. If you have a mass of 70. kg and your SUV decelerates at −5.0 m/s², what will your deceleration be? Explain your answer. _____

   _____

   _____

3. Based on your answer to question 2, what force will your body feel as you stop for the yellow light? _____

   _____

13B INVESTIGATION

Center of Gravity

Objectives

The purpose of this investigation is to

1. Locate the center of gravity of an object.

2. Determine the stability of an object based on the location of its center of gravity.

Materials

Paper
String
Styrofoam™
Tape
Thread
Thumbtack

Equipment

Forks (2)
Hanger
Laboratory mass
Mounting block
Thumbtack
Wooden block

Introduction

As you learned in your textbook, two objects exert a gravitational force on each other that is proportional to their masses. The gravitational force exerted by an object draws the matter surrounding it toward a point located in the exact center of mass of the object. We call this point the **center of gravity (c.g.).** The location of the c.g. is important for determining the *stability* and the *balance point* of an object, concepts that will be discussed later. For simple geometric objects, even three-dimensional ones, locating the c.g. is relatively easy. If you assume that mass is uniformly distributed throughout the object, then the c.g. is located at its geometric center. For example, the center of gravity of a sphere is located at the intersection of two or more diameters of the sphere (see A, below). The c.g. of a rectangular block is located at the point of intersection of the diagonal lines extending from one corner through the block to the opposite corner (see B, below). The c.g. of a cylinder is at the midpoint of a line passing through the centers of the circles at the ends of the cylinder (see C, below).

A.   B.

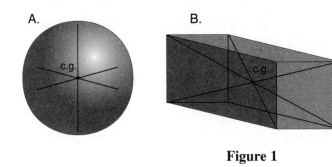

C.

Figure 1

The c.g. of irregular objects can be found experimentally by using a device called a *plumb line or bob.* This is a builder's aid that determines the line of the force of gravity at a given location. It is used to ensure that the walls of buildings are vertical (plumb) during construction. When an object is suspended, the point of suspension and its c.g. lie in the line of gravity. If you attach a plumb bob to the point of suspension, the plumb line will pass through the location of the object's c.g. While this will work theoretically for all objects using an imaginary plumb line, in practice it is useful only for two-dimensional (flat) objects because a string will not pass through the center of a three-dimensional solid. If you suspend a flat object at two or more points and trace the lines of gravity, they will intersect at the c.g. (see Figure 2).

Figure 2

The location of the center of gravity of an object is directly related to its stability. A **stable** object will return to its original position if tilted. An **unstable** object will tumble until it arrives at a new stable position different from the original. Your own experience will demonstrate this. You are in a stable position walking along the sidewalk. If you trip, however, you become unstable and fall. After you have stopped tumbling, you are again stable, but you are now in quite a different position. Stability is determined by the relative positions of an object's c.g. and its **support base.** The support base of an object is the two-dimensional surface that supports a three-dimensional object. One example would be the base of a pyramid. The support base can also be a one-dimensional edge or side that supports a two-dimensional object such as a triangle. As long as the c.g. of the object lies on a vertical line that passes through the object's base, the object will retain some stability. If the c.g. is moved to a point that lies outside of the object's base of support, the object will fall over. When it comes to rest, it will have a new base and the c.g. will again lie above the base.

Stability is related to two factors: the vertical distance of the c.g. from the base and the length of the base. Changing either of these factors affects the stability of an object. For example, lowering the c.g. and increasing the length of the base both increase stability for the same reason; you must tip the object farther before the c.g. falls outside of the base.

Pre-Laboratory Questions

Read the entire investigation. Answer the following questions prior to class on a separate sheet of paper. Use complete sentences.

1. What is the point in an object called toward which the masses of all other objects are attracted?

2. Where is this point located?

3. What assumption must be made to find the c.g. geometrically?

4. What determines the stability of an object?

5. What common carpentry tool will you use to find the center of gravity of a hanger?

6. If the center of gravity were lowered below the base of support or the fulcrum of an object, how stable would it be?

7. Which vehicle would be more stable, a Formula 1 racing car or a large SUV? Explain your answer.

Procedures

A. Locating the Center of Gravity

As discussed earlier, the center of gravity of a two-dimensional object can be found by using a plumb line that is simply a weight attached to a string.

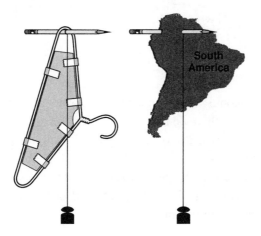

Figure 3

1. Cut a piece of paper to the size of the open space of a clothes hanger. Tape the paper so that the open space is covered. Leave a gap at the two corners large enough to insert a pencil.

2. Tie some thread to the weight and secure the other end of the thread to a pencil. Make sure that the pencil-to-weight distance is longer than the coat hanger.

3. Insert the pencil at one of the corners of the hanger and allow it to hang so that the thread lies against the paper. Without disturbing the position of the hanger or thread, mark several points along the thread on the paper, then lay the hanger on a table and connect the dots using a ruler to reconstruct the position of the thread.

4. Repeat step 3 twice, suspending the hanger first from the other corner and then from the hook at the top.

5. The three pencil lines should intersect at the center of gravity.

6. Try to balance the hanger on the eraser of a pencil placed at the center of gravity. Does it balance? _____

_____

Sometimes a town claims to be the geographic center of that country or state. This claim can be verified by cutting out the shape of the country and locating the center of gravity using this same method. Be sure to make the holes large enough that the pattern can hang freely from the pencil (see Figure 3).

B. Stability

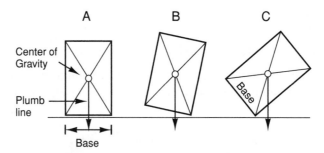

Figure 4

1. Draw two diagonal lines connecting opposite corners on the end of a wooden block with a pencil and a ruler. Be as accurate as possible. Assuming the block is uniform through its length, the point of intersection lies on an imaginary line through the middle of the block. The c.g. is at the midpoint of this line in the geometric center of the block. Therefore, we can use the intersection of diagonals at the end of the block to represent the position of the center of gravity.

2. Set the block at the edge of a table or desk. Insert a thumbtack into the intersection of the two diagonals you drew. Tie the plumb line to the thumbtack so that it can hang freely.

3. Rock the block slightly onto a corner so that the plumb line falls within the base as in B above. Release the block.

   a. Did the block return to its original position? _____

   b. Was the block stable? _____

4. Tip the block again, this time making sure that the plumb line is beyond the base as in C above.

   a. Did the block return to the original position? _____

   b. Was the block stable? _____

   c. How would you describe the relative height of the c.g. when the block is completely stable and when it becomes unstable? _____

   _____

   _____

C. Optional Demonstration of Stability

Humans have a smaller base of support than four-footed animals because humans have only two feet. Humans and animals alike, however, must keep their centers of gravity above their bases of support to remain stable.

1. With your feet together, place a pencil on the floor just in front of your toes. Without moving your feet and keeping your legs straight, bend over to pick up the pencil off of the floor. Notice how your shoulders move in front of your feet and your hips move backward to compensate.

   a. Were you able to pick up the pencil? _____

   b. Did your center of gravity remain above your base of support? How do you know? _____

   c. Were you stable? _____

2. Stand with the back of your shoes against a wall and try to repeat the same procedure.

   a. Were you able to pick up the pencil? _____

   b. Did your center of gravity remain above your base of support? Explain.

   _____

   c. Were you stable as you leaned forward? _____

D. Increasing Stability

Let us consider a teeter-totter (which is basically a plane supported at its center along a line) or a spinning top (which is supported by a single point). Either will be stable only when supported at its *balance point* (or fulcrum). Additionally, in order for it to be completely stable, the mass of the object must be distributed in such a way that its c.g. lies in a vertical line directly *below* its balance point. If the c.g. is in any other location, the object will be unstable and will tend to rotate around the balance point until it falls. If the c.g. is in a vertical line directly above the fulcrum, the object is completely unstable and its motion will be unpredictable. In the two examples mentioned, the legs of the riders of the teeter-totter lower the c.g. of the entire system below the fulcrum. The top maintains temporary stability through gyroscopic forces, but when it slows too much, it falls to its side, which provides a larger base. Increasing the distance of the c.g. below the fulcrum increases stability because it increases the force that tends to return the object to its original position.

In the investigation below, you will observe the effects of changing the location of the center of gravity of an object relative to its balance point.

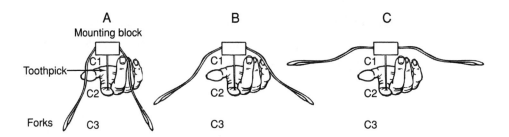

Figure 5

1. Obtain a mounting block of styrofoam or other material, two forks, and a toothpick.

2. Insert the two forks and the toothpick into the mounting block as shown in A of Figure 5, above. To start with, the middle of the fork handles should be below the free end of the toothpick. Attempt to balance the assemblage by placing the end of the toothpick on your fingertip.

   a. Did the assemblage balance? _____

   b. Is the assemblage stable? _____

   c. Referring to A in Figure 5, is the c.g. of the assemblage at C1, C2, or C3? _____

   d. Is this above or below the point of support? _____

   _____

   e. Slightly tip the assemblage. Describe what happens when you release it.

   _____

   f. Describe the relative heights of the c.g. of the assemblage before you tipped it and the c.g. at its maximum angle before you released it.

   _____

   _____

   g. What inference can you make about the relationship between height of c.g. and stability? _____

3. Insert the two forks into the mounting block at increasingly wider angles, as shown in B and C. Attempt to balance the assemblage in each case.

   a. Could you balance the assemblage in every case? _____

   b. When you *could* get the assemblage to balance, was it more or less stable than in question 2 of this part? _____

   c. When the assemblage falls, what seems to be the relative height of the c.g. of the assemblage compared to the balance point? _____

   _____

4. Referring to Figure 5, which center of gravity position (C1, C2, or C3) was the most stable? _____

5. Which was the least stable? _____

6. What was the point of support? _____

_____

7. How did raising the center of gravity compared to the base of support affect the stability of the assemblage? _____

8. Does this support the inference you made in question 2 of this part?

_____

Discussion Questions

1. Where would you expect to find the center of gravity of a wheel? _____

_____

2. How does the size of the support base of a cow compare with the base of a human? _____

3. Explain why it is easier for a four-footed animal to learn to walk than a human. _____

_____

4. What happens to your center of gravity when you carry a loaded backpack?

_____

How do you compensate for this change? _____

5. How does the *height* of the c.g of a fully loaded log truck compare to that of an empty log truck? _____

How would this affect the truck's stability? _____

6. Which shape in Figure 6, below, would be the most stable: A, B, or C? Why? _____

7. Which vehicle in Figure 6 would be more stable, D or E? Why? (Assume that the width of the trucks and of their tires is the same.) _____

_____

_____

Figure 6

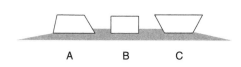  

A   B   C   D   E

8. What features of a military Humvee (Hummer) make it more stable than a regular car? _____

_____

9. A tightrope walker often carries a heavy, flexible pole whose ends droop below the level of the tightrope. Why does this make his job easier?

_____

10. Sir Isaac Newton demonstrated that two objects do not have to be physically connected to have a common center of gravity. If you consider the earth and moon as a system, would the system's center of gravity be located at point A, B, C, or D in Figure 7? _____ The earth and moon together revolve around their common center of gravity.

Earth   Moon

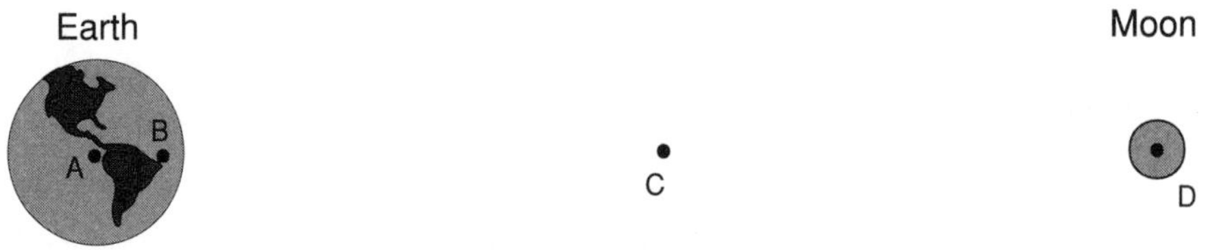

Figure 7

11. Based on your conclusion from question 10, if you threw a hammer, would it rotate around point A, B, C, or D in Figure 8? _____

_____

Figure 8

Objectives

The purpose of this exercise is to

1. Review some basic concepts of levers.
2. Verify that the law of moments ($w_1 d_1 = w_2 d_2$) holds true for any first-class lever.

Equipment

Knife-edge clamp
Mass hanger clamps (2)
Mass set
Meter stick
Support stand
Unknown mass

Introduction

If you had to open a can of paint, which of the following would you prefer to use: A quarter, a brass key fob, or a screwdriver? Why?

The answer is, of course, that you have "more leverage" with the screwdriver. What does this actually mean? You have learned about the law of moments and the structure of a first-class lever. Let's apply that knowledge to opening the can of paint. There are three physical parts of a lever system. They are the resistance arm (the distance of the resistance force from the fulcrum), the effort arm (the distance of the moving force from the fulcrum), and the fulcrum (the pivot point around which the lever arms rotate). The two non-physical components of a lever system are the resistance and effort forces. In our paint can problem, the resistance arm is the distance from the can rim to the underside edge of the lid, the fulcrum is the can rim, and the effort arm is the distance from the rim to the end of the tool you choose to use. The resistance is constant for each case, amounting to several hundred pounds of frictional force between the lid and the can. The effort force depends to some extent on how good a grip you can get on the tool. The coin can be gripped only with fingertips, while the key fob and the screwdriver can be gripped with the whole hand.

Before we attempt to "open the can," we need to discuss the concept of **torque.** A torque is the product of the force acting perpendicularly to a lever arm rotating around a fulcrum and the distance between the fulcrum and the point of application of the force. (See Figure 1, right.) The word *torque* itself comes from the Latin word meaning "to twist." Every time you unscrew a cap from a jar or bottle, you are exerting a torque. A torque is also called a **moment.** A first-class lever and, for that matter,

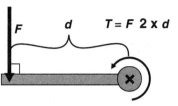

Figure 1: Torque (*T*)

any lever, consists of two torques working against each other. You have learned that for a change in motion to occur, an unbalanced force must be applied to an object. Motion around a fulcrum occurs only with unbalanced torques. In order to open the paint can, the effort torque (the force that you exert times the distance between the can rim and the end of your tool) must exceed the resistance torque (the frictional force of the can lid times the small distance from the can rim to the underside of the lid).

If there is no motion of a lever around a fulcrum, then how do the torques compare? The *torques* must be equal. This does not necessarily imply that the forces or the lever arms involved are equal. When this situation occurs, we say the lever system is in **equilibrium.** We will use this principle in our study of the first-class lever.

Pre-Laboratory Questions

Read the entire investigation. Answer the following questions prior to class on a separate sheet of paper. Use complete sentences.

1. Define in your own words the following terms:

    a. law of moments

    b. torque

    c. equilibrium

2. How many torques are applied in every simple lever system?

3. How do you calculate the weight of an object if you know its mass in kilograms?

4. How do you know that a lever system is in equilibrium?

5. If a lever system is in equilibrium, what do you know must be true about the torques acting on the lever?

6. Why must you balance the meter stick first before adding any masses to it?

7. How do you find the mechanical advantage (M.A.) of a first-class lever system?

Procedures

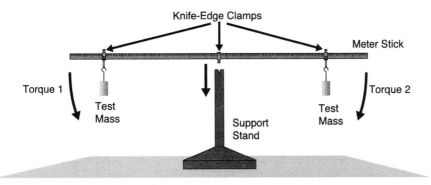

Figure 2: Lever Arm Assembly

Assemble the Apparatus

1. Slide the knife-edge clamp onto the meter stick to the 50 cm mark and gently tighten the screw.

2. Set the meter stick lever assembly onto the support stand and check the balance.

3. If the meter stick does not come to rest horizontally, loosen the set screw and move the stick toward the high end. Repeat until the stick balances horizontally.

4. Slide the mass hangers onto the lever assembly so that the wire hangers are below the meter stick, but do not tighten.

Identify Masses

1. Obtain the hooked or slotted masses to be used in this investigation.

2. Label the two 50. g masses **A** and **B.** Label the 100. g mass **C** and the 200. g mass **D.**

3. Write each mass in grams in the left column of Table 1 adjacent to the corresponding letter. If the masses you are using are different from those listed, then substitute as required. Assume their masses are precise to the nearest gram.

4. Convert each mass to kilograms in the middle column.

5. Calculate their weights by multiplying by 9.81 N/kg and write this value in the right-hand column.

6. Write the masses' weights in the corresponding blocks in Table 2.

Table 1: Test Masses

Mass Letter	Grams	Kilograms	Newtons
A	g	kg	N
B	g	kg	N
C	g	kg	N
D	g	kg	N

Trial 1—Using Two Equal Masses

1. Hang mass **A** 40.0 cm (0.400 m) to the left of the fulcrum. (Refer to Figure 2.) All masses that will produce Torque 1 (the resistance) in this and the following trials should be hung on the left side of the fulcrum.

2. In Table 2, multiply the weight of mass **A** by 0.400 m (d_1) to obtain the torque for mass **A**. Enter this value in the table under $w_1 d_1$. Be sure to observe proper significant digits for all calculations if your teacher requires you to do so.

3. On the other side of the apparatus, hook mass **B** to the hanger and slide the hanger until the lever balances horizontally.

4. Measure the distance of mass **B** from the fulcrum to the nearest 0.1 cm. Convert the measurement to meters and record it in the column labeled d_2 for Trial 1. (**Note:** Record all distances in Table 2 in meters.)

5. Multiply the weight of mass **B** by d_2 to find the torque for mass **B** (the effort). Write this value in the column under $w_2 d_2$ for Trial 1.

6. Carefully remove the masses from the lever arm.

Trial 2—Using Two Unequal Masses

1. Hang mass **C** at 20.0 cm (0.200 m) from the fulcrum. Assume that this is the *effort*. Calculate $w_2 d_2$ for mass **C** and enter this value in Table 2 for Trial 2.

2. On the other side, hook mass **A** to the hanger and slide it until the lever balances horizontally.

3. Determine the distance d_1 for mass **A**. Complete Table 2 for Trial 2.

4. Remove the masses from the lever arm.

Trial 3—Using Specified Arms with Various Masses

1. Hang mass **D** at 30.0 cm (0.300 m) from the fulcrum. Calculate $w_1 d_1$ for mass **D**.

2. On the other side of the lever, tighten the empty hanger 40.0 cm (0.400 m) from the fulcrum.

3. Experiment with various combinations of masses **A** through **C** until one is found that brings the lever into balance, or nearly so.

4. Record the mass letters under w_2 for Trial 3 and add the corresponding weights from Table 1. Write the total weight in the w_2 block.

5. Complete Table 2 for Trial 3.

6. Remove the masses from the lever arm.

Trial 4—Determining the Weight of the Unknown Mass

1. Hang mass **D** at 20.0 cm (0.200 m) from the fulcrum. Calculate w_1d_1 for mass **D.**

2. On the opposite side, hook the unknown mass on the hanger and adjust its position until the lever system balances horizontally.

3. Record the distance of the unknown mass from the fulcrum under the d_2 column for Trial 4.

4. Since the lever system is in equilibrium, to what value must the torque w_2d_2 be equal? _____

5. Estimate the weight of the unknown mass using the law of moments as follows:

   law of moments: $w_1d_1 = w_2d_2$ weight of unknown $= w_2$

   solve for w_2: $w_2 = \dfrac{w_1d_1}{d_2}$

   $w_2 =$ _____

6. Complete Table 2 for the unknown mass.

Results

Table 2: First-Class Levers

	Resistance Arm			Effort Arm		
Trial	w_1	d_1	w_1d_1 Torque 1	w_2	d_2	w_2d_2 Torque 2
1	N	0.400 m	N·m	N	m	N·m
2	N	m	N·m	N	0.200 m	N·m
3	N	0.300 m	N·m	N	0.400 m	N·m
4	N	0.200 m	N·m			N·m

Discussion Questions

1. What is the torque of the resistance arm in Trial 1? _____

2. What is the torque of the effort arm in Trial 1? _____

3. Compare the torque of the resistance and effort arms in the other trials. What does this comparison tell you about the law of moments? _____

   _____

   _____

4. What will happen if the torques are not equal? _____

5. The mechanical advantage (M.A.) of a machine indicates how easy or hard it is to move the resistance. It is a measure of how much the simple machine multiplies the effort force. One way it can be determined is by finding the ratio of the resistance force to the effort force $\left(\text{M.A.} = \dfrac{R}{E}\right)$.

Find the M.A. for the levers in Table 2 of this investigation $\left(\text{M.A.} = \dfrac{w_1}{w_2}\right)$.

a. Trial 1 _____

b. Trial 2 _____

c. Trial 3 _____

Notice that with first-class levers, the M.A. may be less than, greater than, or equal to 1, depending upon the position of the fulcrum. However, a first-class lever is not useful if its M.A. is less than 1.

6. Trial 1 corresponds to lever B in Figure 3, below, since the resistance arm and lever arm are the same length. The M.A. is _____ (from question 5), which means that the lever does not make the resistance any easier or harder to move.

7. Trial 2 corresponds to lever C. The M.A. is [greater] [less] than 1, which means that the lever makes the resistance [easier] [more difficult] to move. (Circle the correct answers.)

8. Trial 3 corresponds to lever A, below. The M.A. is [greater] [less] than 1, which means that the lever makes the resistance [easier] [more difficult] to move.

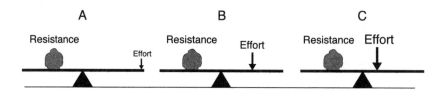

Figure 3: Various Combinations of Forces

9. The M.A. can also be found by comparing the effort arm (d_2) with the resistance arm (d_1). Give the M.A. for the trials using the ratio M.A. $= \dfrac{d_2}{d_1}$.

a. Trial 1 _____

b. Trial 2 _____

c. Trial 3 _____

10. Compare these values to the values in question 5.

    a. What can be said about these two ratios (w_1/w_2 and d_2/d_1)?

    _____

    b. Set up a proportion with these two ratios.   _____

    c. Cross-multiply the proportion.   _____

    d. What do you call the resulting equation?

    _____

Experimental Evaluation

11. Use Figure 2 for reference.

    a. In Trial 1, which direction would Torque 1 rotate the lever arm? _____

    _____

    b. In the same trial, which direction would Torque 2 rotate the arm? _____

    _____

    c. How do the magnitudes of the two torques in Trial 1 compare? _____

    _____

    d. What do we call a quantity that has both magnitude and direction? _____

    _____

    e. What kind of quantity is a torque? _____

12. Your observations are recorded in Table 2. From these observations and the conclusion from question 11, what inferences can you make about the torques for a balanced lever? The torques on a balanced lever are _____ in magnitude but _____ in direction.

13. Theoretically, the torque of the resistance and effort arms should have been the same. Realistically, should you expect the two values to be identical? Explain. _____

    _____

    _____

    _____

14. This generalization can be applied to all levers, but can this be proved? Explain. _____

    a. Can we achieve the second objective of this investigation? _____

15. (Optional) What are the units of torque? _____

    a. What other quantity have you learned about that has units of N·m?

    _____

    b. Is this the same thing as torque? Explain your answer. _____

    _____

    _____

    _____

14B INVESTIGATION

Second- and Third-Class Levers

Objectives

The purpose of this exercise is to

1. Demonstrate the applicability of the law of moments to second- and third-class levers.

2. Determine the mechanical advantage of various lever systems.

Equipment

Knife-edge clamps, 4
Lever apparatus support
Meter stick
Metric mass set or equivalent
Spring balance, 10 N
Unknown masses

Introduction

Investigation 14A demonstrated the applicability of the law of moments to the first-class lever. The law of moments shows that the torque on one side of the fulcrum (w_1d_1) must be equal to, but in the opposite direction from, another torque (w_2d_2) if the lever arm is to be in equilibrium (motionless and balanced). Recall that torques are vector quantities, but the law of moments we use shows only the scalar values for these torques. This is an acceptable simplification for this level of instruction. The law of moments may be written in a more general form of $F_1d_1 = F_2d_2$. In this version, *any* force, not just a weight, acting perpendicular to a distance from a pivot or axis can create a torque. This is the principle by which an engine can apply rotational force to a drive shaft.

In the first-class lever, the torques are arranged on opposite sides of the fulcrum. In second- and third-class levers, however, the torques are both on the same side of the fulcrum. Does the law of moments still hold true in these cases? We will answer this question during this investigation.

To review the arrangements of the various classes of levers, examine Figure 1, below, and answer the following questions. Diagram A represents a first-class lever because the fulcrum is between the resistance and the effort. Diagram B represents a _____-class lever because the _____ is between the _____ and the _____. Diagram C represents a _____-class lever because the _____ is between the _____ and the _____.

A   B   C
Resistance   Effort   Resistance   Effort   Effort   Resistance

Fulcrum   Fulcrum   Fulcrum

Figure 1

Pre-Laboratory Questions

Read the entire investigation. Answer the following questions prior to class on a separate sheet of paper. Use complete sentences.

1. In general, what is a torque?

2. Give an example of a torque you might use in your home.

3. How do you prepare the spring balance to measure force for this investigation?

4. What must you do in this investigation to compensate for the weight of the two hangers on the left side of the fulcrum?

5. Due to the construction of the third-class lever apparatus, what must be done differently from the other levers when taking data?

6. State a research question for this investigation.

Procedures

A. Assemble the Second-Class Lever Apparatus

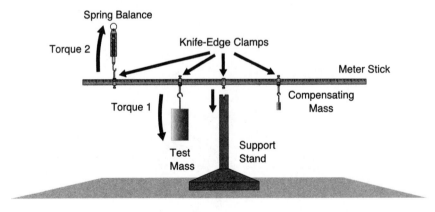

Figure 2

1. Obtain the equipment listed for this investigation and assemble the fulcrum clamp, the meter stick, and the stand according to Figure 2. Note that the fulcrum clamp does not have a mass hanger.

2. Balance the apparatus as you did in Investigation 14A. Gently tighten the clamp.

3. This investigation requires that both the resistance (Torque 1) and the effort (Torque 2) be on the same side of the fulcrum. Install the two knife-edge clamps on the left side of the fulcrum as shown in Figure 2. Do not tighten these clamps until required to do so in the following sections.

   a. What happened to the lever arm after you installed the clamps in step 3?

   _____

   b. Is the lever arm in equilibrium at this point? Explain. _____

   _____

4. Slide an additional clamp and hanger onto the right arm. This will be used to hang a compensating weight on the right arm to offset the additional weight of the two clamps/hangers on the left arm during the trials in the following sections.

5. Hold the spring balance vertically by the upper ring. Do not hook the balance to any weights for this check. Examine the location of the pointer compared to the zero point of the scale. If the pointer is not at zero, slide the scale up or down until the pointer is exactly on zero. This step is called *zeroing* the balance. Zeroing before taking a measurement is done for many kinds of scientific instruments.

B. Identify the Masses

1. Obtain the 500. g and the 200. g masses to be used in this investigation.

2. Write each mass in grams in the left column of Table 1. If the masses you are using are different from those listed, then substitute as required. Assume their masses are precise to the nearest gram.

3. Convert each mass to kilograms in the middle column.

4. Calculate their weights by multiplying by 9.81 N/kg and write this value in the right-hand column.

5. Write the weight for the 500. g mass in the F_1 column in Table 2 for Trials 1-3. Write the weight for the 200. g mass in the F_1 column in Table 3 for Trials 1-3.

Table 1: Test Masses

Grams	Kilograms	Newtons
g	kg	N
g	kg	N

C. Second-Class Lever Trials

Trial 1

1. Slide the mass hanger closest to the fulcrum on the **left** arm to a point 10.0 cm (0.100 m) from the fulcrum. Gently tighten the clamp. If the meter stick did not balance with the fulcrum exactly at the 50.0 cm mark, do not simply clamp the hanger at the 40.0 cm (or 60.0 cm) mark but measure 10.0 cm from the actual balance point.

2. Slide the outermost clamp (with the hanger on top) on the **left** arm to a position 40.0 cm (0.400 m) from the fulcrum and tighten the clamp.

3. Note that the lever arm is not in equilibrium. Hook a 10 g mass on the **right-hand hanger** and slide it to a position where the lever is balanced. If a 10 g mass cannot balance the lever with the clamp at the extreme right end of the lever, balance the lever with the next larger mass.

4. With the clamps in position and the lever balanced, hook a 500. g mass to the inner hanger and the spring balance to the outer hanger on the left arm as in Figure 2.

5. Lift the spring balance until it is supporting the left arm of the lever. The 500. g mass must be off of the table, and the lever should be approximately horizontal.

6. Read the spring scale force in newtons to one-tenth of the smallest (decimal) graduation. Record this value as F_2 in Table 2 for Trial 1.

7. Unhook all masses and the spring scale from the lever.

8. Calculate Torque 1 and Torque 2 by multiplying the corresponding weights and lever arms. Record the results in Table 2 for Trial 1.

Trial 2

1. Loosen the left-most clamp and slide it to a point 30.0 cm (0.300 m) from the fulcrum and tighten.

2. Hook the compensating mass on the right-hand hanger and adjust its position until the lever arm balances. Tighten the clamp.

3. Hook the 500. g mass and the spring balance to the hangers as in Figure 2 and record the force needed to lift the left end of the lever arm to the equilibrium position as in Trial 1.

4. Record this value as F_2 in Table 2 for Trial 2.

5. Unhook all masses and the spring scale from the lever.

6. Complete Table 2 for Trial 2.

Trial 3

1. Loosen the left-most clamp and slide it to a point 20.0 cm (0.200 m) from the fulcrum and tighten.

2. Repeat the remaining steps as before for Trial 1.

3. Unhook all masses and the spring scale from the lever.

4. Complete Table 2 for Trial 3.

Trial 4 (Unknown Weight)

1. Loosen the left-most clamp and slide it to a point 40.0 cm (0.400 m) from the fulcrum and tighten.

2. Balance the lever arm as before.

3. Hook the unknown mass to the innermost hanger on the left arm.

4. Hook the spring balance to the outermost hanger as before and measure the force necessary to lift the lever arm to equilibrium. Record this as F_2 for Trial 4 in Table 2.

5. Determine the weight of the unknown.

   a. Calculate the magnitude of Torque 2 (F_2d_2). _____

   b. If the lever was in equilibrium, what must be true about the *magnitudes* of Torque 1 and Torque 2? _____

   _____

   c. Write an equation that will allow you to solve for the weight of the unknown. _____

   _____

   d. Solve for F_1 in Trial 4. _____

   _____

D. Results—Second-Class Levers

Table 2: Second-Class Levers

	Resistance Arm			Effort Arm		
Trial	F_1	d_1	F_1d_1 Torque 1	F_2	d_2	F_2d_2 Torque 2
1	N	0.100 m	N·m	N	0.400 m	N·m
2	N	0.100 m	N·m	N	0.300 m	N·m
3	N	0.100 m	N·m	N	0.200 m	N·m
4	N	0.100 m	N·m	N	0.400 m	N·m

E. Third-Class Levers

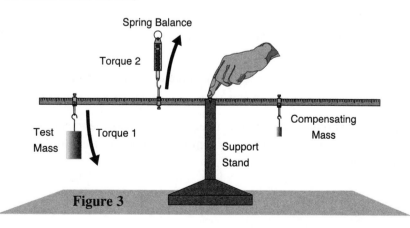

Figure 3

Assemble the Apparatus

1. Rearrange the lever apparatus by swapping the positions of the hanger clips on the left-hand clamps. The hanger of the innermost clamp should be on top of the meter stick, and the left-most hanger should be below the meter stick.

2. The 200. g mass will be used for the known mass trials in this section.

Trial 1

1. Position the left-most hanger at 40.0 cm (0.400 m) from the fulcrum. Position the inner hanger at 10.0 cm (0.100 m) from the fulcrum.

2. Balance the lever with the compensating mass as before in Section C.

3. Hook the 200. g mass to the outermost hanger on the left. Hook the spring scale to the innermost hanger. See Figure 3.

4. Place a fingertip on the fulcrum clamp directly above the support stand. As you raise the spring scale to lift the lever arm, you will need to press down on the fulcrum just enough to prevent it from pulling out of the support. Do not exert so much force that you twist the lever arm with your finger.

5. Note the force on the spring scale required to lift the lever arm. Record as F_2 in Table 3 for Trial 1.

6. Unhook all masses and the spring scale from the lever.

7. Complete Table 3 for Trial 1.

Trial 2

1. Position the innermost hanger on the left to a point 20.0 cm (0.200 m) from the fulcrum.

2. Repeat the remaining steps as before in Trial 1 of this section.

3. Complete Table 3 for Trial 2.

Trial 3

1. Position the innermost hanger on the left to a point 30.0 cm (0.300 m) from the fulcrum.

2. Repeat the remaining steps as before in Trial 1 of this section.

3. Complete Table 3 for Trial 3.

Trial 4 (Unknown weight)

1. Position the innermost clamp on the left to a point 20.0 cm (0.200 m) from the fulcrum.

2. Balance the lever arm as before with the compensating mass.

3. Hook the unknown mass to the left-most hanger.

4. Hook the spring balance to the innermost hanger as before and measure the force necessary to lift the lever arm to equilibrium. Record this as F_2 for Trial 4 in Table 3.

5. Determine the weight of the unknown.

    a. Calculate the magnitude of Torque 2 (F_2d_2). _____

    b. Solve for F_1 in Trial 4 as in Section C. _____

    _____

F. Results—Third-Class Levers

Table 3: Third-Class Levers

	Resistance Arm			Effort Arm		
Trial	F_1	d_1	F_1d_1 Torque 1	F_2	d_2	F_2d_2 Torque 2
1	N	0.400 m	N·m	N	0.100 m	N·m
2	N	0.400 m	N·m	N	0.200 m	N·m
3	N	0.400 m	N·m	N	0.300 m	N·m
4	N	0.400 m	N·m	N	0.200 m	N·m

Discussion Questions

1. The mechanical advantage (M.A.) of a machine indicates how easy or hard it is to move the resistance. One way M.A. can be determined is by finding the ratio of the resistance to the effort. In this investigation, the ratio would be F_1/F_2. Complete the following table to determine the M.A. of second- and third-class levers using the forces recorded in Tables 2 and 3.

Table 4: Mechanical Advantage

Trial	Second-Class M.A.	Third-Class M.A.
1		
2		
3		

    a. The mechanical advantage of a second-class lever is always _____ than one. This means that using a second-class lever to raise an object is [harder] [easier] than simply picking it up.

    b. The mechanical advantage of a third-class lever is always _____ than one. This means that using a third-class lever to raise an object is [harder] [easier] than simply picking it up.

2. In the investigations with levers we were concerned with weight (or force) applied to the levers instead of mass.

   a. What is the difference between weight and mass? _____

   _____

   _____

   b. Why was force (i.e., weight) used in this investigation instead of mass?

   _____

   _____

   _____

3. Review the values of the resistance torques compared to the effort torques in Tables 2 and 3. How do their magnitudes compare? _____

   _____

4. Since the lever arm was in equilibrium for each trial, compare the directions of the resistance and effort torques. _____

   _____

5. Examine the apparatus for the third-class lever test in Figure 3. Can you explain why it is necessary to hold down the fulcrum during the test? (Hint: Compare the downward force exerted by the test mass compared to the upward force exerted by the spring balance.) _____

   _____

   _____

   _____

Experimental Evaluation

6. Would it be possible to prove that the law of moments applies *exactly* to any given lever? Explain your answer. _____

   _____

   _____

7. (Optional) If you have not done so, read page 330 of your textbook. Discuss why it is not critically important that a law of science such as the law of moments produce exact results. _____

   _____

   _____

   _____

   _____

   _____

8. (Optional) Scientific laws are used to predict various effects, but they do not explain what causes these effects. For example, the law of gravity can be used to predict the motion of most of the planets around the sun, but it says nothing about why the sun attracts the planets or how that attraction reaches to the planet. From questions 6 and 7, write in your own words two limitations of the laws of science. _____

_____

_____

Objectives

The purpose of this exercise is to

1. Demonstrate the mechanical advantage of an inclined plane.

2. Gain practice in mathematically solving for variables in a formula.

3. Investigate the behavior of physical quantities as a limit is approached.

Materials

Masking tape
String

Equipment

Board
Kinetic cart
Metric masses
Metric ruler
Spring balance (20 N)

Introduction

One of the most useful simple machines is the inclined plane. This has been in use since the earliest days of human history. It was used to construct huge structures such as the pyramids. It can be found in edge tools and weapons such as chisels and war axes. It was used by the American pioneers to fell trees and then to split the wood with wedges. Every screw and bolt has an inclined plane wrapped around a cylinder or cone. The inclined plane works by supporting some of the load as the load is moved through a distance by the effort. The more of the load that the inclined plane takes, the easier it is to move.

Simple machines are useful because they boost the effects of the user's efforts. This is called mechanical advantage (M.A.). As we have shown in previous investigations, you can find the M.A. of a machine by dividing the resistance force by the effort force $\left(\text{M.A.} = \dfrac{R}{E} \right)$. In a basic inclined plane, you would divide the weight of the object you were moving up the plane by the effort it took to move it. Inclined planes exhibit another rule that applies to all simple machines—the distance principle. This rule states that when using a simple machine, the reduction in the amount of force required to move a resistance is accompanied by a proportionately larger distance that the effort must act through. For an inclined plane, the M.A. can be calculated by dividing the length of the plane by the vertical distance that is gained as you move from the bottom to the top of the plane $\left(\text{M.A.} = \dfrac{L}{h} \right)$. For example, if a ramp is 3 m long and you rise 1 m as you walk from one end to the other, then the M.A. is $\dfrac{3\ \cancel{m}}{1\ \cancel{m}} = 3$. Once you know the M.A. of a specific inclined plane, you can use that information to predict the effort required to move the resistance. In the example above, if the load to be moved is 150 lb., then the effort will be only 50 lb. $\left(E = \dfrac{R}{M.A.}\right)$, ignoring friction.

In this investigation, we will be using the experimental principles you have learned in the past to demonstrate the mechanical advantage of the inclined plane and exploring some mathematical properties of these relationships.

Pre-Laboratory Questions

Read the entire investigation. Answer the following questions prior to class on a separate sheet of paper. Use complete sentences.

1. Give two methods for determining the mechanical advantage of an inclined plane.

2. What is the rule that relates the magnitude of the effort and the distance it must act through in order to move the resistance?

3. If the M.A. of a ramp is 4 and its length is 12 m, what is the height of the ramp?

4. If an object weighs 400 N, how much effort will it take to push it up the ramp in question 3?

5. What are the units of M.A.?

6. In this investigation, does the kinetic cart have to be moving in order to demonstrate the mechanical advantage of the inclined plane? Explain your answer.

7. Why is it a good idea to average several readings of the same measurement together when collecting data?

8. If an inclined plane rises 2 m and is 4 m long, then it can be said that for every meter of upward motion, you must move ? m along the inclined plane.

Procedures

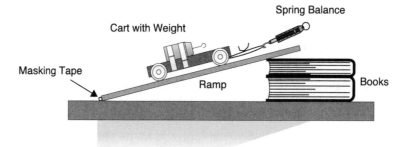

Figure 1

A. Setup

1. Tape a 1000. g mass to a kinetic cart using masking tape.

   In the next step, you will measure the weight of the cart and mass. One or two other individuals should make the same measurement without sharing the results until all have made the measurement. This ensures independence of the measurements and avoids bias. Use this method whenever the instructions say to independently make a measurement.

2. Zero the 20 N spring balance as discussed in Investigation 14B. Carefully hook the cart to the balance and measure the weight of the cart and mass to the nearest 0.1 N.

   a. If the cart does not have a convenient way to hook to the balance, tie some string around an axle in a loop and hook the balance into the loop. Make the loop large enough so that it extends beyond the end of the cart.

   b. Record the weights in the blanks:

   Your measurement: _____

   Partner 1 measurement: _____

   Partner 2 measurement: _____

   Average: _____

   c. Write the average weight in every blank in the "Cart Weight" column in the data table.

3. Independently measure the length of the board to be used as a ramp to the nearest 0.01 cm.

   a. After your partners have measured the board, enter the values in the blanks below and find their average.

   Your measurement: _____

   Partner 1 measurement: _____

   Partner 2 measurement: _____

   Average: _____

   b. Write the average measurement in every blank in the "Ramp Length" column in the data table.

4. When setting up the ramp, it is important to ensure that it does not move during the measurements. If this happens, the height will change, making the data invalid. Tightly roll up several lengths of masking tape so that the sticky surface is outward. Press the rolls of masking tape firmly onto the table along the base of the ramp. This will prevent the ramp from sliding away from the books.

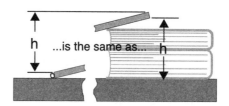

Figure 2

B. Trial 1

1. Set up the ramp on a stack of two books as in Figure 1. If the table has a square edge along its top surface, place the ramp parallel to and right at the edge of the table. This will make measuring the height easier.

2. Independently measure the height of the ramp perpendicular to the tabletop. Since the bottom surface of the ramp rests on the table, it is easier to measure the height from the tabletop to the underside of the raised end of the ramp. See Figure 2, above.

   a. Examine the lower end of your metric ruler before making this measurement. If there is a metal end cap on the meter stick or if the end has been damaged, measuring from the end will not give you an accurate measurement. Place a convenient mark on the meter stick such as 10.00 cm at the tabletop and measure from that point to the underside of the ramp. Subtract 10.00 cm from your reading to find the height.

   b. If the procedure in a. is not possible because the table has a rounded edge and your ruler's scale cannot be accurately read at the end, measure the height of the **upper** surface at the *base* of the ramp and the **upper** surface at the *top* of the ramp. Subtract the first measurement from the second to obtain the height.

   c. After your partners have measured the ramp height, enter the values in the blanks below and find their average.

      Your measurement: _____

      Partner 1 measurement: _____

      Partner 2 measurement: _____

      Average: _____

   d. Write the average measurement in the blank in the "Ramp Height" column for Trial 1 in the data table.

3. Find the M.A. of the ramp by dividing the ramp length by its height $\left(\text{M.A.} = \dfrac{L}{h} \right)$. Observe correct significant digits (SDs) if your teacher requires; otherwise, report the result to the nearest tenths place. Write this value in M.A. column for Trial 1 in the data table.

4. Estimate the effort required to hold the cart in equilibrium on the ramp using the M.A. determined in step 3. Recall from the introduction that $E = \dfrac{R}{\text{M.A.}}$. Divide the weight of the cart by the M.A. and enter this value in the "Predicted Effort" column for Trial 1 in the data table.

5. Independently measure the effort to hold the cart in equilibrium on the ramp. Place the cart on the middle of the ramp, hook the spring balance to the cart or the loop of string, and measure the force to the nearest 0.1 N.

   a. After your partners have measured the effort, enter the values in the blanks below and find their average.

      Your measurement: _____

      Partner 1 measurement: _____

      Partner 2 measurement: _____

      Average: _____

   b. Write the average measurement in the block under "Measured Effort" for Trial 1 in the data table.

C. Additional Trials

1. More trials can be taken using additional books. Repeat steps 1-5 under Trial 1 for taking and recording data.

2. If there is time, you may want to try the extreme cases of the ramp horizontal and the ramp vertical. These situations will be considered in the discussion questions.

Results

Data: Inclined Planes

Trial	Cart Weight	Ramp Length	Ramp Height	M.A.	Predicted Effort	Measured Effort
1						
2						
3						
4						
5						

Discussion Questions

1. Answer the following questions by referring to Figure 3.

   a. What is the M.A. of the inclined plane? _____

   b. Based on your answer in part *a,* for every meter that the load moves vertically, the load moves _____ m along the ramp.

   c. If the height of the ramp were 10 m, what would be the length of the ramp? _____

   d. If it requires 1000. N of force to move a load along the ramp, what would be the weight of the load? _____

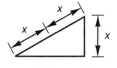

Figure 3

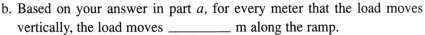

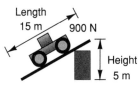

Length
15 m   900 N

Height
5 m

Figure 4

2. Answer the following questions by referring to Figure 4.

   a. What is the M.A. of the ramp? _____

   b. In other words, for every 1 m the cart moves vertically, it moves _____ m along the ramp.

   c. How much force would be required to hold the cart stationary on the ramp? _____

   d. How much work would be required to lift the cart vertically 5.0 m? ($W = F \cdot d$) _____

   e. How much work would be required to push the cart 15 m along the ramp with 300. N of force? _____

   f. Does the ramp reduce the work required to move the cart a certain vertical distance? Explain your answer. _____

   _____

   _____

   g. What does the ramp reduce? _____

   _____

   h. What does the ramp increase when moving the cart? _____

   _____

4. (Optional) It is sometimes instructive to examine extreme cases, and you may have tested these in Part C of the Procedures, above. Let us examine the case when the inclined plane is vertical.

   a. If the ramp is vertical (length of the ramp equals the height of movement), what would be the M.A.? _____ If you were to move a 1000. N load up this "ramp," you would use a _____ effort.

   b. Is there any advantage to using a vertical ramp? _____

   _____

Chapter 14

5. (Optional) Suppose the ramp is horizontal. (The change in height from one end to the other is zero.)

   a. The M.A. of a 15 m ramp would be _____. Does this value exist?

   _____

   b. To avoid dividing by zero, you can examine the M.A. as the height becomes smaller and smaller. Calculate the M.A. in the following cases. What will happen to the M.A. when the height becomes extremely small, so small that you cannot measure it any more ($h = 0$)?

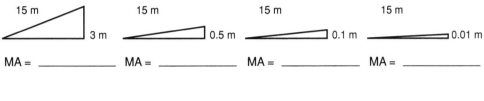

MA = _____ MA = _____ MA = _____ MA = _____

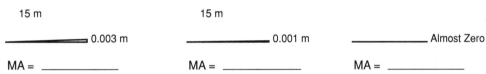

MA = _____ MA = _____ MA = _____

   c. Does a horizontal ramp provide any advantage to lift a load? _____

   _____

Experimental Evaluation

6. Is it possible to obtain an exact measurement for the length of the board?

   _____

7. (Optional) Why would the force required to move the cart up the ramp at a constant speed be slightly larger than the force required to hold the cart still on the ramp? Give one of two possible reasons. _____

   _____

   _____

   _____

   _____

   _____

   _____

15A TEACHER DEMONSTRATION

Pressure

Objectives

The purpose of this exercise is to demonstrate

1. The presence and effects of atmospheric pressure.
2. The relationship of water pressure to depth.
3. Some properties of flowing fluids.

Introduction

This exercise is based on the material presented in your textbook. You should recall that *pressure* is defined as the amount of force applied over a certain area (force/area). The SI unit for pressure is called the **pascal** (Pa). One pascal is equal to one newton per square meter ($1 \text{ Pa} = 1 \text{ N/m}^2$).

Demonstrations

I. Pressure

A. Air Pressure

Would you allow someone to place 14,000 lb. of weight on you? You probably wouldn't. Believe it or not, however, this is approximately the force of normal air pressure on an average-sized person. The total force that the air exerts on you can be calculated by multiplying the atmospheric pressure (air pressure at sea level is 14.7 lb./in.^{2}) by the number of square inches of your surface area (skin). This force does not crush us because God designed our bodies to function under these conditions. The matter in our bodies exerts a pressure in the outward direction equal to the force of the atmosphere pressing in on us. As long as these forces are balanced, we feel no ill effects. The pressures are said to be in a state of equilibrium. You probably have noted air pressure changes in your ears or sinuses. These sensations occur when the pressures on opposite sides of membranes in your body are not in equilibrium.

The relationships between gas pressure, temperature, and volume are described by two equations known as Boyle's law and Charles's law. You will be studying these laws in more detail in a later exercise. Boyle's law states that as the pressure exerted on a sample of gas increases, the volume will decrease, assuming constant temperature. In other words, a gas can be compressed by exerting pressure on it. Charles's law states that as the temperature of a sample of gas increases, its volume will increase, assuming constant pressure. These two laws acting together can produce dramatic effects on sealed objects containing a gas. For example, if the internal pressure of a non-rigid sealed object is raised because the temperature increases, the volume of the object will tend to increase.

1. ***"Suction"***   Observe as your teacher performs the demonstration with the flask and the hard-boiled egg.

    a What did the teacher do? _____

    _____

    _____

    b. What happened? _____

    _____

    c. Explain the results. _____

    _____

    _____

    _____

    _____

    _____

2. ***Crush the Can***   Observe as your teacher performs the demonstration with the aluminum can.

    a. What did the teacher do? _____

    _____

    b. What happened? _____

    c. Explain the results. _____

    _____

    _____

    _____

    _____

B. Air Pressure and Density

The density of an object determines whether it will float or sink in a fluid. If the density of the object is greater than the surrounding fluid, it will sink.

1. ***Atmospheric Buoyancy*** Observe as your teacher performs the demonstration with the balloon and the meter stick.

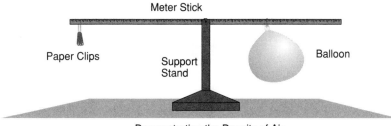

Meter Stick

Paper Clips   Balloon

Support
Stand

Demonstrating the Density of Air

a. What did the teacher do? _____

_____

_____

_____

_____

b. What happened? _____

_____

c. How do you think the density of the air inside the balloon compared to the density of the air in the room? _____

_____

_____

d. Explain the results. _____

_____

_____

_____

e. Discuss why good experimental design required that your teacher inflate the balloon, deflate it, and place it on the balance before he performed the demonstration? _____

_____

_____

2. **_Cartesian Diver_**   Observe as your teacher performs the demonstration with the Cartesian diver.

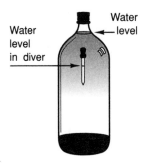

Water level in diver

Water level

a. What did the teacher do? _____

_____

b. What happened? _____

_____

_____

c. How did the density of the eyedropper change when the teacher squeezed the bottle? _____

_____

d. Explain the results. _____

_____

_____

_____

_____

_____

_____

_____

II. Water Height and Gravity

The pressure in a body of water differs according to the depth at which you measure the pressure in the water. The water molecules at the surface of the liquid experience only the pressure of the air above them. The water molecules at the bottom of the body of water are under more pressure because they experience the weight of all of the water molecules above them as well as the air pressure above the water. The pressure experienced is directly related to the height of the water above that point. This increase in pressure is one reason that water towers are built on hills and usually have leg supports to raise the tanks even higher. This is also why submarines can be crushed if they go below a certain depth.

1. **_Deeper Means Higher_**   Observe as your teacher pulls the tape off the plastic bottle.

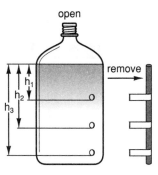

a. Describe the bottle used in this demonstration. _____

_____

b. What did your teacher do? _____

_____

_____

c. Describe what happened. _____

_____

d. Explain the results. _____

_____

_____

_____

e. If your teacher had turned the bottle on its side before taking off the tapes, would the results have been the same? Explain. _____

_____

_____

2. ***The Lower It Goes, the Faster It Flows***   Observe as your teacher demonstrates the use of a siphon.

a. Describe the apparatus used in this demonstration. _____

_____

_____

_____

b. What happened? _____

_____

c. Explain the results.

(1) What kind of energy is associated with the height of an object?

_____

_____

(2) How does this kind of energy at the higher end of the siphon compare with the energy at the lower end? _____

_____

_____

(3) What is happening to the energy of the water as it flows from the higher pan to the lower container? _____

(4) What principle states that all processes naturally proceed toward the lowest energy and highest disorganization? _____

_____

d. If you reversed the positions of the containers halfway through the demonstration, what would happen? _____

_____

e. Would the results of this demonstration change if the bend in the tube was raised? _____

_____

III. Moving Fluids

Both flowing air and flowing water exhibit many of the physical properties that are characteristic of all fluids. These properties are studied together under the heading **fluid pressure.** Bernoulli recognized that the pressure a moving fluid exerts is directly related to the speed at which that fluid is flowing. The faster the fluid is flowing over a surface, the lower the pressure that the fluid exerts on that surface. Air and water are fluids, so they both demonstrate this property. This simple observation has led to some amazing technology. Powered flight, sailing vessels, hydrofoils, motorboats, sail planes, kites, and Frisbees all depend on Bernoulli's principle.

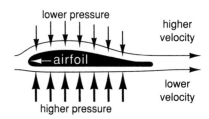

Observe as your teacher demonstrates the Bernoulli effect discussed in your textbook.

a. What did the teacher do? _____

_____

b. What did you observe? _____

_____

c. Explain the results. _____

_____

_____

Discussion Questions

A. Pressure

Molecules moving at the surface of a liquid must have a certain amount of kinetic energy to enter the gas above the liquid because the gas molecules, with much higher kinetic energies, are pressing down on the liquid surface. The force that a liquid must exert at its surface in order to become a vapor is called **vapor pressure.** Vapor pressure of a liquid increases as the liquid is heated. Water boils only when its vapor pressure equals or exceeds atmospheric pressure. At sea level, the air pushes down on the liquid surface at about 10^5 Pa. As you increase altitude (you are at a shallower "depth" in the atmosphere), the atmospheric pressure decreases. Because there is essentially no atmosphere in space, the pressure is very near 0 Pa. With this information answer questions 1 to 4.

1. Water boils at 100°C at sea level. Explain why water boils below 100°C at higher altitudes. _____

_____

_____

_____

2. Could liquid water exist in space outside a spacecraft? Explain. _____

   _____

3. What would happen to the blood of an astronaut if he were not in a pressurized environment? _____

   _____

4. A pressure cooker is sealed so that it generates pressure inside the pot higher than the surrounding atmospheric pressure. Explain why the water in a pressure cooker boils at a temperature higher than 100°C. _____

   _____

   _____

   _____

5. If the atmosphere applies 10^5 Pa of pressure on your skin, how much pressure does your skin apply to the atmosphere? _____

6. Car brakes use liquids to transfer and amplify the force from your foot to the brake. Considering Pascal's principle, why is it dangerous to get air in the hydraulic piping of the brake system? _____

   _____

   _____

B. Working with Pressure (Pascals)

One pascal is defined as one newton applied over a square meter $\left(P = \dfrac{\text{Force}}{\text{Area}} \Rightarrow \dfrac{\text{N}}{\text{m}^2} \right)$. Recall that weight $= \text{mass} \times g \Rightarrow \dfrac{\text{kg·m}}{\text{s}^2}$, where g is the acceleration due to gravity (9.8 m/s^2).

Keeping these relationships in mind, answer the following questions.

1. If a breeze pushes on a two-square meter door with a total force of 60 N, how much pressure (in pascals) has been applied?

   Formula: _____

   Substitute: _____

2. The water in a ten-gallon aquarium weighs 360. N. How much pressure will be applied to the bottom of the aquarium if the bottom measures 0.30 m by 0.60 m?

   Find the area of the base: _____

   Formula: _____

   Substitute: _____

15B INVESTIGATION
Buoyancy

Name _____

Date _____   Hour _____

Objectives

The purpose of this exercise is to

1. Gain practice making measurements and calculating density.

2. Make predictions from theory and experimentally test the predictions.

Materials

Corn oil
Glycerol
Green food coloring

Equipment

Eyedroppers (2)
Graduated cylinder, 10 mL
Mass balance
Test tube brush
Test tubes (3)
Test tube rack

Introduction

The relative ease with which a fluid can support an object is called **buoyancy.** Buoyancy of an object is directly related to its density. You have read in your textbook about Archimedes' principle. Archimedes' principle states that an object is supported by a force that is equal to the weight of the fluid displaced. If you submerge a wooden block in water, as we did in Investigation 3D, and measure the volume of water displaced by the block, you will find that the weight of the water displaced was greater than the weight of the wooden block. This is the reason that the block float: the buoyant force upward is greater than the force exerted downward by the weight of the block. If an object has a density greater than water, the weight of the object is greater than the buoyant force and the object sinks. Finding the density of an object by measuring the weight and volume should allow you to predict whether an object will sink or float in water. A steel ship is able to float despite its great weight because it contains an enormous volume, most of which is air. Its overall density is much lower than that of water.

Density is a physical property of all matter. Different liquids have different densities. In this investigation you will be calculating and comparing the densities of corn oil and glycerol with the density of water. Based on your results, you will be able to predict if these substances will float or sink in the presence of the others.

Pre-Laboratory Questions

Read the entire investigation. Answer the following questions prior to class on a separate sheet of paper. Use complete sentences.

1. What is the buoyant force on an immersed object equal to?

2. In which direction does the buoyant force act?

3. To which property of an object or substance is buoyancy directly related?

4. Why does a steel ship float even though the density of the metal is much greater than that of water?

5. If you forgot the density of water, how could you determine it?

6. Why do you add green food coloring to the water in Part A of the procedure?

Procedures

A. Water

1. Place 5.0 mL of water in a test tube.

2. Add 1 or 2 drops of green food coloring into the water in the test tube. Set the tube aside. Record the density of water in the data table below.

B. The Density of Corn Oil

1. Find the mass of the 10 mL graduated cylinder. Record this in ① below.

2. Pour 5.0 mL of corn oil into the graduated cylinder. Add the last few tenths of a mL dropwise to avoid overshooting.

3. Find the combined mass of the graduated cylinder and the corn oil. Record this in ② below.

4. Find the mass of the corn oil by subtracting 1 from 2 and write the answer in ③ below.

    ② Mass of the cylinder and corn oil   _____

    ① Mass of the cylinder   − _____

    ③ Mass of the corn oil   = _____

5. Calculate the density of the corn oil and record that value in the data table (Density = mass/volume).

6. Pour the corn oil into a second test tube.

7. Clean the graduated cylinder using soap and a test tube brush and dry.

8. Record the density of corn oil calculated by two other groups in the data table.

9. Calculate and record the average density of corn oil for all three groups.

C. The Density of Glycerol

1. Record the mass of the 10 mL graduated cylinder in ④ below.

2. Pour 5.0 mL of glycerol into the graduated cylinder. Using a clean eyedropper, add the last few tenths of a mL dropwise to avoid overshooting.

3. Find the combined mass of the graduated cylinder and the glycerol. Record this in ⑤ below.

4. Find the mass of the glycerol by subtracting ④ from ⑤ and write the answer in ⑥ below.

⑤   Mass of the cylinder and glycerol   _____

④   Mass of the cylinder   − _____

⑥   Mass of the glycerol   = _____

5. Calculate the density of the glycerol and record that value in the data table.

6. Pour the glycerol into a third test tube.

7. Clean the graduated cylinder with soap and a test tube brush and dry.

8. Record the density of glycerol calculated by the two other groups in the data table.

9. Calculate and record the average density of glycerol for all three groups.

D. Order of Layers

1. Predict which substance will be the …

top layer   _____

middle layer   _____

bottom layer   _____

2. Pour the corn oil into the test tube that contains the water. Do not shake the test tube.

3. Pour the glycerol from the graduated cylinder into the same test tube. Record the order of layers in the data table.

4. Clean all glassware with soap and water and dry thoroughly.

Data Table: Density

Substance	Density (g/mL)				Order of Layers (top, middle, bottom)
	Your Group	Group 2	Group 3	Average	
Water					
Corn Oil					
Glycerol					

Discussion Questions

1. How can you predict whether a substance will float without placing it into water? _____

2. In both the Dead Sea and in the Great Salt Lake, a person is able to float on the surface and raise both hands and both feet out of the water. How is the water in these two lakes different from fresh water? _____

_____

3. Why does that affect your ability to float? _____

_____

_____

4. Gasoline has a density of 0.67 g/mL. Will gasoline float on top of a layer of water or sink underneath its surface? _____

_____

5. What will happen if you try to use water to put out a gasoline fire? _____

_____

Experimental Evaluation

6. Why were the densities for corn oil and glycerol determined by the three groups not exactly the same? _____

_____

_____

7. Did your experiment match your predictions? _____

_____

8. Did this investigation prove that *everything* with a density less than 1 g/mL will float in water and *everything* with a density greater than 1 g/mL will sink? Explain. _____

9. (Optional) The density of a water strider is greater than 1 g/mL, yet it is able to walk on the surface of a pond. Why do you think that the insect can do this? _____

_____

10. (Optional) If the water strider were pushed beneath the surface of the water, what would happen to it? _____

11. (Optional) This investigation assumed that the density of the tap water you used was 1.0 g/mL (the density of pure water). Do you think this is a correct assumption? Explain. _____

_____

12. (Optional) Is this assumption about the density of water acceptable for this investigation? Would it be acceptable for scientific research? Explain both questions. _____

_____

_____

_____

Objective

The purpose of this exercise is to gain experience in solving problems involving changes in pressure, volume, and temperature of a sample of an ideal gas.

Introduction

While this is principally a math exercise, it will also give you some practical experience in deciphering word problems. The key to solving word problems is to focus first on what you are required to find. Then note what you are given or what is known. After you have correctly done these two steps, identifying the required formula is fairly easy. Gas law problems are straightforward proportions if you can identify which quantities go with which variables. Just remember that any words such as *initially, former, original,* or *before the change,* refer to quantities with a subscript of 1. Similarly, any words such as *final, new,* or *after the change,* refer to quantities with a subscript of 2. Unknown quantities may have either subscript. So it is important to list your known and unknown quantities at the beginning of the problem and assign them variables. (Computer programmers almost always assign variables at the beginning of their programs.)

It is more important to understand the physical process than to be able to "turn the equation crank" to get the correct answer. After each problem, look at the change in the given quantities and note how the unknown quantity responded. This is a good way to check your solution. If the change does not follow the gas law, then you probably have made an error.

A. Boyle's Law

Boyle's law states that as the pressure exerted on a given amount of a gas increases, the volume of the gas decreases. This kind of relationship between two such properties is called an inverse proportion. Boyle's law is expressed by the formula $P_1V_1 = P_2V_2$.

Example: 4.0 L of a gas is at a pressure of 500. mm Hg. If the pressure is doubled, what will be the new volume?

Follow these steps:

1. Known information: $V_1 = 4.0$ L, $P_1 = 500.$ mm Hg, $P_2 = 1000.$ mm Hg

2. Required quantity: $V_2 = ?$

3. Write the applicable formula: $P_1V_1 = P_2V_2$

4. Rearrange the equation and solve for the desired variable. In this case, you are trying to find V_2:

$$V_2 = \frac{P_1V_1}{P_2}$$

5. Substitute known values into the equation: $V_2 = \dfrac{500.\text{ mm} \times 4.0\text{ L}}{1000.\text{mm}}$

6. Solve the problem: $V_2 = 2.0$ L

Solve the following problems writing out the six steps given in the example. Assume that the temperature remains constant in each case.

1. 5.2 L of a gas is at 200. mm Hg pressure. What will be the new volume if the pressure is reduced to 100. mm Hg?

2. 8.0 L of a gas is initially at 400. mm Hg pressure. If the gas is allowed to expand to 10. L in volume, what is the final pressure?

3. What will be the new volume of a gas at the new pressure of 1500. mm Hg if the gas had an initial volume of 12 L at 750. mm Hg pressure?

4. You currently have 24 L of a gas at 800. mm Hg pressure. If the *original* pressure of the gas was 400. mm Hg, what was its *original* volume?

B. Charles's Law

Charles's law states that as the temperature of a sample of gas increases, the gas volume increases, assuming that the pressure remains constant. This kind of relationship between two properties is called a direct proportion. Charles's law is expressed by the formula $\frac{V_1}{T_1} = \frac{V_2}{T_2}$, where T is measured in kelvins (K). Give a mathematical reason that you could not use the Celsius temperature. _____

_____

_____

_____

Example: A gas initially has a volume of 4.0 L at 200. K. If the temperature is doubled, what will be the new volume, assuming pressure remains constant?

Follow these steps:

a. Known information: $V_1 = 4.0$ L, $T_1 = 200.$ K, $T_2 = 400.$ K

b. Required quantity: $V_2 = ?$

c. Write the applicable formula: $\frac{V_1}{T_1} = \frac{V_2}{T_2}$

d. Rearrange the equation and solve for the unknown variable. In this case we are solving for V_2: $V_2 = \frac{V_1 T_2}{T_1}$

e. Substitute known values into the equation:

$$V_2 = \frac{4.0 \text{ L} \times 400. \text{ K}}{200. \text{ K}}$$

f. Solve the problem: $V_2 = 8.0$ L

Solve the following problems. Write out the six steps given in the example. Assume that pressure remains constant for each situation.

1. Given 5.2 L of a gas at 300. K, what will be the new volume if its temperature is reduced to 150. K?

2. Given 8.0 L of a gas at 250. K, what will be the *change* in temperature $(T_2 - T_1)$ if the new volume after the change is 16 L?

3. Determine the new volume of a sample of gas at 600. K if its initial volume was 12 L at 400. K.

4. The volume of a gas at 400. K is 16 L. If the original volume was 10. L, what was the original temperature?

Boyle's and Charles's Law

Name _____

Date _____ Hour _____

Objective

The purpose of these demonstrations is to help the students understand the differences between temperature, heat, and thermal energy through practical experiences.

Introduction

The terms *temperature, heat,* and *thermal energy* are often used incorrectly. However, each has a specific definition. **Temperature** is a measure of the average kinetic energy of the molecules in a substance. The temperature is not dependent on the number of particles present (the mass of the substance). The concept of "measure" relies on a numerical system that is directly proportional to the kinetic energy. *Average* kinetic energy implies that not all of the particles of matter are necessarily moving at exactly the same speed. Some of the molecules are moving faster than the average and some slower. **Thermal energy** is the measure of the total kinetic energy of all the particles of the substance. Thermal energy is therefore dependent on the total mass of the object. Although *heat* and *thermal energy* are often used interchangeably, **heat** refers only to the *transfer* of thermal energy from one place to another. You can discuss how much heat was given off or absorbed by a substance, but it isn't proper to discuss how much heat is contained in a substance.

Procedures

I. Temperature

A. Sensory Perception

When your skin comes in contact with an object or substance, your nerve endings seem to give you a sense of how hot or cold the object or substance is. However, these sensory perceptions are dependent on many different factors and they can easily deceive us. With prolonged contact, the sensors lose their responsiveness and you no longer feel the initial temperature difference so intensely. This can be illustrated with a frog. If the frog is dropped into very hot water, it will immediately leap out of the pan. However, if the frog is placed in lukewarm water and the water is heated slowly, the frog will not notice the change in temperature and will remain in the water until the hot water kills it.

Watch as one of your classmates places one index finger in a cup of cold water and the other in a cup of hot water.

How does he describe the intensity of the sensation of temperature after leaving his fingers in the cups for five minutes? _____

_____

How does he describe the sensation of temperature when he places both index fingers in the cup of water at room temperature? _____

_____

_____

Is your fingertip a reliable temperature indicator? _____

Questions

1. If you spend too much time in the snow without proper protection, your feet will start feeling very cold. What happens to the sensation of coldness if you ignore the feeling and stay outside? _____

_____

2. Have your feet warmed up or are you getting inaccurate sensory information from your feet? _____

_____

3. Could this "lack of feeling" be dangerous? Explain. _____

_____

B. Measuring Temperature

Our senses do not provide an objective way to measure temperature. The Facet on pages 360–61 in your textbook provides the history of the development of the modern temperature scales and thermometers that allow us to measure temperature objectively and with great precision. Liquid thermometers indicate temperature by the liquid level in a fine tube calibrated in degrees. The level depends on the liquid volume as it expands and contracts in response to an increase or decrease of the average kinetic energy of the fluid. The kinetic energy of a distinct, physical object can be calculated easily, but the average kinetic energy of the *particles* in a substance cannot be measured directly in joules. By using a calibrated scale to measure the expanding fluid in a thermometer, we can *infer* the magnitude of the average kinetic energy of a substance without actually measuring it.

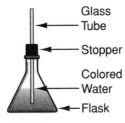

Observe the level of water in the tube as your teacher heats the demonstration flask. What did you observe? _____

Questions

1. Both Gabriel Fahrenheit and Anders Celsius divided their scales between two temperatures they believed to be fixed into 100 divisions. State the fixed points used for each scale. _____

_____

_____

2. Why do you think Fahrenheit used mercury instead of pure water as the liquid in his thermometer? _____

_____

3. Does a thermometer directly measure particle kinetic energy? _____

_____

_____

4. Upon what physical property does a thermometer depend? _____

_____

_____

5. When you measure temperature, does the reading imply that all of the molecules of that substance are moving at exactly the same speed? Explain.

_____

_____

II. *Heat and Thermal Energy*

Several principles are important when talking about heat and thermal energy. First, all matter has thermal energy, even substances that we consider "cold." Unless the substance is at absolute zero, the molecules have some kinetic energy. Second, when two objects or substances touch, their molecules collide with each other transferring kinetic energy to the other substance. Therefore, heat is actually flowing in both directions. However, the net heat flow is from the hotter object or substance to the colder one. When both objects are the same temperature or the temperature of the two substances is constant, they are said to be in *thermal equilibrium*. Heat transfer has not stopped at that point; it merely proceeds at the same rate in both directions.

When a substance is undergoing a phase change (melting or boiling), it is possible to add heat without increasing the temperature of a substance. The added heat provides the energy to disrupt the various bonds that hold the molecules together in the less energetic state.

A. Heat

Observe the two cups of water that your teacher presents to the class. One cup is near the boiling point of water; the other is at room temperature.

1. What is visibly different about them? _____

_____

2. As the steam rises, what is being transferred to the air? _____

3. Why is the heat moving in this direction? _____

_____

_____

4. Is there any heat flow associated with the cooler cup of water? _____

5. Which direction(s) is the heat flowing? _____

_____

6. Is there any net heat flow? Explain. _____

_____

7. What is this condition called? _____

B. Thermal Energy and Mass

Trial 1: Your teacher will mix 50 mL of boiling water with 50 mL of water at room temperature in a Styrofoam cup.

1. Enter the temperatures of the hot and cold water as given by your teacher in the data table.

2. Make a prediction of the temperature of the mixture.

3. Enter the actual temperature of the mixture as measured by your teacher.

Trial 2: Your teacher will mix 75 mL of boiling water with 25 mL of water at room temperature in a Styrofoam cup.

1. Enter the temperatures of the hot and cold water in the data table as given by your teacher.

2. Make a prediction of the temperature of the mixture.

3. Enter the actual temperature of the mixture as given by your teacher.

Table 1: Thermal Energy and Mass

	T_{hot}	m_{hot}	T_{room}	m_{room}	Predicted T of Mixture	Actual T of Mixture
Trial 1		50 g		50 g		
Trial 2		75 g		25 g		

Questions

1. Was the actual temperature of the mixture in Trial 2 higher or lower than in Trial 1? _____

2. Why were the actual temperatures different? _____

_____

_____

3. In which trial was more thermal energy added to the mixture? _____

_____

4. Was the temperature of the hot water in each trial different? _____

5. Explain how the amount of thermal energy was increased. _____

_____

_____

6. What is the relationship between temperature and thermal energy?

_____

_____

_____

C. Thermal Energy and Phase Changes

1. Boiling

Observe the temperature as your teacher applies heat for several minutes to water that is already boiling.

Temperature

Initial _____

1 min. _____

2 min. _____

3 min. _____

4 min. _____

5 min. _____

a. Can thermal energy be added to an object or substance without increasing its temperature? _____

b. When can this happen? _____

_____

c. What is the added thermal energy accomplishing? _____

_____

_____

2. Freezing

Trial 1: Your teacher will mix 50 mL of ice-cold water with 50 mL of water at room temperature.

a. Enter the temperatures of the room-temperature water and the cold water in Table 2 as given by your teacher.

b. Make a prediction of the temperature of the mixture.

c. Enter the actual temperature of the mixture as given by your teacher.

Trial 2: Your teacher will mix 50 g of ice with 50 mL of water at room temperature.

a. Enter the temperatures of the ice and the water in the data table as given by your teacher.

b. Make a prediction of the temperature of the mixture.

c. Enter the actual temperature of the mixture as given by your teacher.

Table 2: Thermal Energy in Different Phases

		T_{cold}	m_{cold}	T_{room}	m_{room}	Predicted T of Mixture	Actual T of Mixture
Trial 1	Ice Water		50 g		50 g		
Trial 2	Ice		50 g		50 g		

Questions

1. Which trial resulted in a higher temperature? _____

   _____

2. How did the temperatures of the ice water in Trial 1 and the ice in Trial 2 compare? _____

3. Does the ice-cold water have any thermal energy? _____

   _____

4. Which contains less thermal energy, a certain mass of water at 0°C or the same mass of ice at 0°C? _____

   _____

5. Why was the temperature lower in Trial 2? _____

   _____

   _____

Discussion Questions

Write the correct term (*temperature, heat,* or *thermal energy*) in the blanks in the following questions.

1. _____ involves the flow of energy from a hot object to a cooler one.

2. Ice may be cold, but it still has some _____ energy.

3. A measure of the average kinetic energy of the particles of a substance is called its _____.

4. Fifty grams of lead will have more _____ than 1 g of lead at the same temperature.

5. Fifty grams of lead at 75°C will give off more _____ to the atmosphere than 1 g of lead at the same temperature.

6. Hot coffee cools off because _____ is transferred from the coffee to the air.

7. A large iceberg will have more _____ than a small ice cube, although they may have the same _____.

8. (Optional) Thermal energy is defined as the total amount of kinetic energy in the particles of an object. On the surface, this definition appears to answer the question "What is thermal energy?" However, this explanation contains an undefined term, *energy*. Do scientists know what any type of energy *is* or merely how it *behaves*? _____

   _____

   _____

People frequently think that science enables us to fully understand nature. In fact, it often describes only how nature operates. This is knowledge that God has given us to enable us to "subdue the earth and have dominion over it." We should use science as a tool to further God's purposes.

Specific Heat

Objective

The purpose of this investigation is to determine the specific heats of several different metals.

Materials

Paper towels
Styrofoam cups, 8 oz (3)

Equipment

Beaker, 1000 mL
Bunsen burner and lighter
Mass balance
Metal samples (3 different metals)
Stirring rod
Thermometer
Tongs
Tripod
Wire gauze

Introduction

As you learned in your textbook, the **specific heat** (c_{sp}) of a pure material is a distinct physical property. Although there are several ways to define specific heat, one common definition is the amount of thermal energy (calories) needed to raise the temperature of 1 gram of the material 1°C. You remember that temperature is a measure of the average kinetic energy of the individual molecules in a material. The amount of kinetic energy given to the molecules by a certain amount of thermal energy depends on the strengths of the chemical bonds within molecules and the attractive forces between molecules. Thus, each material has a different specific heat because these forces are different for each substance. For example, one gram of water requires the input of 1.00 cal of thermal energy to raise its temperature by 1°C. An identical mass of silver needs only 0.05 cal to experience the same change in temperature.

A material with a high specific heat must absorb a large amount of energy for its temperature to rise one degree Celsius. It also releases large amounts of heat for every degree that it cools. A substance with a low specific heat requires a relatively smaller addition of thermal energy for its temperature to rise the same amount, and it releases a smaller amount of heat for every degree that it cools. In other words, materials that have high specific heats hold more thermal energy for every gram of mass than materials with low specific heats.

This investigation is based upon the law of the conservation of energy. When two substances at different temperatures come into physical contact with one another, thermal energy will flow from the one whose particles have greater kinetic energies (higher temperature) to the one whose particles have lower kinetic energy (lower temperature). When the average kinetic energy of both substances has become equal, the net flow of heat stops. Both substances then exist at a temperature somewhere between the original temperatures. In

Specific Heat

addition, the total amount of thermal energy lost by the hotter substance equals the total amount of thermal energy gained by the colder substance. We will use these principles to determine the specific heat capacity of a metal using an insulated device called a *calorimeter*. From its name you can tell that this instrument allows the measurement of heat flow.

The basic idea behind calorimetry is that heat gained or lost by a substance can be calculated if one knows the mass of the substance, the change in temperature of the substance, and its specific heat capacity (c_{sp}). This is expressed in the equation

$$Q = c_{sp} \cdot m \cdot \Delta T$$

where Q is the heat gained or lost, m is the mass in grams, ΔT is the change in temperature ($T_2 - T_1$), and c_{sp} is the specific heat capacity of the substance.

In calorimetry, you begin with a known quantity of water (m_{water}) at a known temperature ($T_{water\ 1}$). A heated piece of a known amount of metal (m_{metal}) at a known temperature ($T_{metal\ 1}$) is placed into the water in the calorimeter, and the system is allowed to come to thermal equilibrium. When you measure the final temperature (T_2), which is the same for the water and the metal, you can determine the change in temperature (ΔT) for both. We know that the heat gained by the water (Q_{water}) in the calorimeter must be equal to the heat lost by the metal ($-Q_{metal}$) because the total thermal energy in the system cannot change. Therefore,

$$Q_{water} + Q_{metal} = 0$$

$$Q_{water} = -Q_{metal}$$

or

$$(c_{sp} \cdot m \cdot \Delta T)_{water} = -(c_{sp} \cdot m \cdot \Delta T)_{metal}$$

From this expression, you can solve for the unknown, the c_{sp} of the metal.

$$c_{sp\ metal} = \frac{(c_{sp} \cdot m \cdot \Delta T)_{water}}{-(m \cdot \Delta T)_{metal}}$$

We know that the c_{sp} of water is 1.00 cal/g·°C, so this expression is often simplified to

$$c_{sp\ metal} = -\frac{(m \cdot \Delta T)_{water}}{(m \cdot \Delta T)_{metal}} \cdot \frac{cal}{g \cdot °C} \cdot$$

Pre-Laboratory Questions

Read the entire investigation. Answer the following questions prior to class on a separate sheet of paper. Use complete sentences.

1. Define *specific heat.*

2. Which is able to hold more thermal energy per gram, a substance with high or low specific heat?

3. How does the law of conservation of energy help you find the specific heat of the metals in this investigation?

4. How do you determine the initial temperature of the pieces of metal?

5. Why do you blot the metal pieces before placing them into the calorimeter?

6. Why is it important to not splash water out of the calorimeter when placing the metal into it?

7. Which material in the calorimeter gains heat in this investigation?

Procedures

Calorimetry

1. Enter the names of the different metal samples in the "Metal" column in Tables 1, 2, and 3, below.

2. Put 400 mL of water into the 1000 mL beaker. This water volume does not have to be exact.

3. Place the beaker on the wire gauze on the tripod, light the Bunsen burner, and begin heating the water to a boil.

4. Use the mass balance to find the masses of the different metals. Measure to the nearest 0.01 g. Record their masses opposite their names in Table 2.

5. Place all three metal samples into the boiling water.

Do not drop the pieces of metal into the beaker. Use tongs to lower them gently into the water to avoid breaking the bottom of the beaker.

Leave the pieces of metal in the water for 10 minutes.

6. Label three 8-oz Styrofoam cups with the names of the metals being tested and add 50.0 mL (50.0 g) of water at room temperature to each cup.

7. Measure the temperature of the water in each cup and record these values opposite the name of the corresponding metal in Table 1 for T_1 (water).

8. Measure the temperature of the boiling water with a thermometer and enter this value in Table 2 for T_1 (metal).

9. **Perform this step as rapidly as possible.** Remove a piece of metal from the boiling water with tongs, quickly blot it dry on a paper towel, and carefully place it into the cup labeled with the matching name without splashing water out of the cup.

10. Stir the water in the cup with a stirring rod (not the thermometer) every thirty seconds and note the temperature on a piece of scrap paper.

11. When the temperature remains the same for three consecutive readings, thermal equilibrium has been established. Record the temperature in Table 1 for T_2 (water) and T_2 (metal).

12. Repeat steps 9 through 11 for the remaining samples of metal.

13. Calculate ΔT_{water} for each metal and complete Table 1.

14. Calculate ΔT_{metal} for each metal and complete Table 2.

15. Calculate the specific heat of each of the different metals by using the last equation given in the introduction. Record your results opposite the metals' names in Table 3.

16. Record the results from two other groups in Table 3 and find the average for each metal.

Results

Table 1: Heat Gained by Water

Metal	T_1	T_2	ΔT_{water} $(T_2 - T_1)$	Mass (m_{water})	$m_{water} \cdot \Delta T_{water}$
				50.0 g	
				50.0 g	
				50.0 g	

Table 2: Heat Lost by Metal

Metal	T_1	T_2	ΔT_{water} $(T_2 - T_1)$	Mass (m_{metal})	$m_{water} \cdot \Delta T_{water}$

Table 3: Specific Heats

Metal	$c_{sp\ metal}$			
	Your Group	Group 2	Group 3	Average

Discussion Questions

1. State a formula for finding the amount of heat any material will gain or lose with a certain temperature change. _____

2. Calculate Q for the following conditions:

Material	m	ΔT	c_{sp} (cal/g·°C)	Q (in cal)
Copper	1.0 g	3.0°C	0.09	
Copper	10.0 g	−2.0°C	0.09	
Glass	1.0 g	−10.0°C	0.20	
Glass	3.0 g	5.0°C	0.20	
Aluminum	10.0 g	2.0°C	0.22	
Aluminum	2.0 g	−2.0°C	0.22	

3. What is the difference between temperature and thermal energy?

_____

_____

_____

4. Although all the metals had the same T_1, did all the metals contain the same amount of thermal energy? _____

5. On a cool evening following a warm day, which would give off more heat to the atmosphere above it, the ocean (c_{sp} = 1.00 cal/g·°C) or the ground (c_{sp} < 0.5 cal/g·°C), as each cooled 5°C? Explain your answer. _____

_____

_____

6. Which would make a better coolant for a car engine, water (c_{sp} = 1.00 cal/g·°C) or alcohol (c_{sp} = 0.58 cal/g·°C)? Explain your answer. _____

_____

_____

Experimental Evaluation

7. You made some assumptions regarding the apparatus and the procedure in order to make the calculations easier. Name one. _____

_____

_____

_____

8. Would these assumptions tend to make your results higher or lower than their standard values? Explain. _____
_____
_____
_____

9. Did everybody obtain the same results for the same metals? Explain why or why not. _____
_____
_____

10. The specific heat for silver is 0.03 cal/g·°C. Do you think this is an exact value or a close approximation? Explain. _____
_____

Name _____

Date _____ Hour _____

Objectives

The purpose of this exercise is to

1. Develop a practical definition of electricity.

2. Observe the properties of static electrical charges.

Materials

Balloon
Oat cereal piece
Office tape
Paper
Plastic bag
Silk fabric (or fur), small piece
Thread

Equipment

Glass rod
Metal rod
Plastic rod
Support stand and ring

Introduction

Suppose you were asked to define *electricity*. You would probably say that it referred to electrical charges, electrons, electric current, or some other term with the root word *electron*. However, defining the word *electricity* using the root word *electron* does not add any new information. This problem arises because nobody can answer the question "What is electricity?" To bypass this difficulty, scientists simply describe how electricity behaves or operates. This approach is called an **operational definition** since it answers the question "What are the properties of electricity?" rather than "What is electricity?"

The Greek philosopher Thales (630?-546 B.C.) was the first person to systematically investigate electrical phenomena. He found that amber (fossilized tree sap), when rubbed, would attract a variety of objects like fluff, feathers, and dried leaves. William Gilbert (1544-1603) called this property *electricity* since the Greek word for amber was *elektron*. With this information, electricity can now be given a preliminary operational definition. Electricity is that property of attraction that results when objects, such as amber, are rubbed. During this investigation we will expand our operational definition by observing other properties of electricity.

Pre-Laboratory Questions

Read the entire investigation. Answer the following questions prior to class on a separate sheet of paper. Use complete sentences.

1. Why is it difficult to define electricity?

2. When scientists cannot define a term with more basic terms, how do they deal with this problem?

3. What is another scientific term you have studied that cannot be properly defined?

4. Describe one method for creating an electrical charge on an object.

5. What device detects the presence of a static electrical charge described in this investigation?

6. What process physically transfers charges from one object to another?

7. Name the process that produces a temporary charge in an object when another charged object is brought near it.

Procedures

As you perform the following steps, answer the associated questions and record your observations in complete sentences. Try to completely describe your observations in your statements.

A. Frictional Effects

1. Tear five or six small pieces of paper (1 cm²) and place them on the tabletop.

2. Touch the plastic rod to the table or floor. Bring it close to the pieces of paper without actually touching them and observe what happens.

    Observation: _____

    _____

3. Now rub the rod with a silk or fur cloth and bring the rod close to the pieces of paper. Describe what happens.

    Observation: _____

    _____

    _____

4. What had to be done for the rod to attract the paper? _____

    _____

    Did the rod have to touch the paper for attraction to occur?

    Observation: _____

B. Charge

1. Touch the metal rod to the table or floor and bring it close to the paper bits without touching them. Describe what happens.

   Observation: _____

2. Rub the metal rod with a fur or silk cloth and bring it near the pieces of paper. Describe what happens.

   Observation: _____

   _____

3. Obtain a 5 cm piece of clear tape. Fold one of the ends over onto itself to form a nonsticky handle about $1/2$ cm long. Stick the tape down firmly to the table.

4. Using your "handle," pull the tape up quickly and bring it near to the pieces of paper. Describe what happens.

   Observation: _____

Summary: The ability to attract that is acquired by objects through rubbing them is called *charge*. Notice that charge is detected only when *two* objects interact. The influence of charge can be exerted at a distance; it is not necessary for the two objects to actually touch each other.

C. Interactions

1. Forming handles as before, stick two 10-cm pieces of tape onto the table.

2. Quickly pull up the pieces of tape and bring them close together without touching. Describe what happens.

   Observation: _____

   _____

3. Both pieces of tape received their charges in the same way—both were pulled up from the table. You can rightfully assume that they have the same charges or **like charges.** State a property of like charges from your observation in step 2.

   Property: _____

4. Forming handles as before, stick two pieces of tape onto the table, one on top of the other (piggyback).

5. Pull both pieces of tape off of the table together and immediately separate them.

6. Bring the pieces of tape together without touching and describe what happens.

   Observation: _____

   _____

Static Electricity

7. The two pieces of tape received their charges in different ways (one from the table and the other from the first piece of tape). You can rightfully assume that they have different charges or **unlike charges.** State a property of unlike charges from your observation in step 6.

   Property: _____

Summary: It is now possible to describe two ways in which pairs of charges can behave: _____

From our observations, we can now extend the operational definition we started with to include not only the interactive property of *attraction* but also _____.

D. Charge Detector

An *electroscope* is one device used to detect the presence of charges. Traditionally, it is a device consisting of a glass jar or flask with an insulator top penetrated by a metal rod. Inside the jar are two thin leaves of metal attached to the rod so that they can swing freely. Your teacher may show you an electroscope or you may be using one for this investigation. A simple yet effective charge detector can be made with two pieces of tape and a support stand. For the purpose of this investigation, we will assume that you are using the latter apparatus.

1. Charge two 10-cm pieces of tape using the piggyback method as in Section C.

2. Stick both pieces to the support stand near each other so that they hang freely as in Figure 1, below.

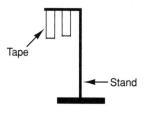

Figure 1

3. Charge a third piece of tape on the table and bring it near both pieces on the charge detector. Describe what happens.

   Observation: _____

4. Remove the pieces of tape from the charge detector.

E. Number of Charges

1. Take two fresh 10-cm pieces of tape and label one **A—Table** and the other **B—Top**. Charge both pieces of tape and stick them to the support stand. When charging or recharging the tapes, always place *A* on the table and *B* on top of *A* as in Section C. It may be necessary to periodically recharge or replace the pieces of tape in this section.

2. Charge various items by rubbing them with the piece of silk or by rubbing them on your hair, shirt, or anything else that will generate friction. Use such things as combs, pens, balloons, Lucite rods, and Bakelite rods, and determine their interaction with tape *A* and tape *B*. Record your results as "attract" or "repel" in the data table.

3. Did any charged object attract or repel both pieces of tape at the same time?

_____

Write a statement that summarizes the possible interactions with tape *A* and tape *B*.

Observation: _____

_____

Summary: Scientists believe that only two charges exist since there are only two states.

Data Table: Electrical Interaction

Charged Object	Interaction (Repel/Attract)	
	Tape A	Tape B

F. Charge by Induction

Up to this point we have produced charges by rubbing or physically transferring charges from one point to another. An uncharged object can acquire a charge when a charged object is brought near to it, even if they don't actually touch. This process is called **induction.** A charge is *induced* when the charged object attracts opposite charges (or repels like charges) in a nearby object, producing one kind of charge on the near surface and the opposite charge on the far surface. Two areas of opposite charges must exist on the second object because it was originally neutral and the charges initially were canceling each other out. Induction is temporary, lasting only as long as the original charged object is present.

1. This demonstration will require a laboratory faucet or a standard sink faucet with the aerator nozzle removed.

2. Establish a very thin stream of water flowing out of the faucet.

3. In Section E, you noted that different kinds of charges can be produced on different objects. Take the same objects used in Section E, charge them again, and bring them near to but not touching the stream of water one at a time. Describe what happens.

Observation: _____

_____

Does the type of charge make any difference in the results? _____

_____

4. Bring a charged rod near the stream of water. Describe what happens.

Observation: _____

If the rod is negatively charged, what must be the charge on the side of the stream of water closest to the rod? Explain. _____

_____

_____

What is the charge of the water stream on the side away from the rod? How do you know this? _____

_____

_____

_____

5. Suspend a piece of toasted oat cereal (e.g., Cheerios) by a thread from the support ring. Bring a charged rod near it (do not allow it to touch!) and describe what happens.

Observation: _____

Assume the rod had a negative charge. Explain why the cereal was attracted to the rod. _____

_____

_____

_____

G. Charge by Conduction

Another way in which a charge may be produced is by using induction to force charges to move from one object to another in contact with it. If the two objects are separated, they will both have a permanent charge. This process is called charging by **conduction.**

1. Bring the charged rod near the suspended piece of cereal. Allow the cereal to touch the rod. Describe what happens.

Observation: _____

_____

_____

2. Try to touch the now-charged cereal with the rod. Describe what happens.

Observation: _____

_____

Assume the rod has a negative charge. Attempt to explain your observations. _____

_____

_____

_____

Discussion Questions

Many people have difficulty understanding electricity and other areas of science because many scientific concepts cannot be defined in distinct, unambiguous terms. We have seen this before with concepts such as energy, gravity, and force. Electricity cannot be defined apart from other electrical terms. This is why scientists resort to operational definitions.

1. What is an operational definition? _____

   _____

2. Give an operational definition for the following terms:

   a. Charge—_____

   _____

   b. Electroscope—_____

   _____

   c. Like charges—_____

   _____

   d. Unlike charges—_____

   _____

   e. Law of charges—_____

Scientists make a number of observations and then state generalizations based upon those observations. In this investigation you made some of the same observations made by the early scientists. You will be asked to make some generalizations based on the indicated observations.

3. Refer to Section A. What did you observe about the relationship between friction and static charges? _____

   _____

4. Refer to Section B. What can you say about acquiring charges on metal and nonmetal objects? _____

   _____

5. Refer to Sections C-E. Give a reason scientists believe there are only two kinds of charges. _____

   _____

   _____

Objects can be charged by conduction or induction. When the cereal piece moved to the rod, it was charged by induction; and when the cereal was repelled by the rod, it had been charged by conduction. The root *duct* has the meaning of a "channel," "passageway," or "path." The prefix *con-* means "with," and the prefix *in-* means "not" or "without." Putting these pieces together, you can see where *conduction* means "a process using a pathway," and *induction* means "a process not using a pathway."

6. Using this information, explain the difference between acquiring a charge by conduction and by induction. _____

_____

_____

_____

_____

7. The word *static* normally means "stationary" and, therefore, can be confusing when the word is associated with static electricity. In some cases the charges are stationary, while in other cases the charges move. Give an example of each that you observed in this investigation. _____

_____

_____

_____

8. Experiments with static electricity work poorly on humid days. Explain the adverse effect of high humidity using the fact that water vapor combines with substances in the air and on surfaces to form electrically charged ions.

_____

_____

17B INVESTIGATION
Circuits

Objectives

The purpose of this exercise is to

1. Demonstrate the properties of current electricity.

2. Demonstrate open circuits, closed circuits, and short circuits.

3. Compare series and parallel circuits.

Materials	Equipment
Masking tape	Alligator clips (2)
Salt	Batteries, 1.5 V (4)
Steel wool	Battery holders (optional) (4)
Sugar	Beakers, 250 mL (3)
Wire, various lengths	Compass
	Conductivity apparatus (see Investigation 2B)
	Insulated shorting wire, heavy
	Knife switch
	Miniature lamps, 6 V (4)
	Miniature lamp base (4)
	Terminal board (optional)
	Voltage test meter (optional)

Introduction

Static electricity deals with charges that are normally considered stationary, although they can jump as a spark, leak into the air on a humid day, or be transferred between objects. *Current electricity* deals with charges that are in continual motion. For a charge to be in motion, two things must be present: a driving force (electrical potential energy) and a path or circuit.

Three types of circuits are the open circuit, the closed circuit, and the short circuit. A closed circuit consists of an energy source (battery or generator), wires or other conductors that form a continuous path, and a load (an object that uses or dissipates most of the energy transferred in the circuit). The load can be a light bulb, speaker, motor, or heating element on a stove, as well as many other devices. An open circuit (which is not really a circuit) lacks the continuous path because there is a gap in the conductor, either purposely made (an open switch) or unintentionally (a break in a wire). A short circuit bypasses the load, so the energy from the driving force is expended only in the wire. This produces very high currents that cause the wire to get hot and melt due to the resistance in the wire.

We will also look at two simple circuit configurations mentioned in your textbook, series circuits and parallel circuits. In series circuits, all electrical charges pass through all electrical components one at a time in a series. The electrical potential energy of the source is used step-wise in each component until it is completely gone at the last load. In *parallel circuits,* the charges take different paths through the various loads. If you arrange the loads side by side in a diagram, the electrical paths through them are parallel. The total electrical potential energy from the source is applied to each component all at the same time.

Pre-Laboratory Questions

Read the entire investigation. Answer the following questions prior to class on a separate sheet of paper. Use complete sentences.

1. What is the difference between static electricity and current electricity?

2. What must exist for current electricity to occur?

3. List the parts of a basic electrical circuit.

4. What kind of device allows us to purposely open a circuit?

5. Can any object be a conductor in a circuit? Explain your answer.

6. What do we call a substance that can conduct electricity in a solution?

7. Name another action-at-a-distance force other than the electrostatic force that is related to electricity.

Procedures

This investigation will be performed at different stations unless you are given other instructions by your teacher. Read the instructions for each station carefully before you begin. After you have completed the actions at a station, be sure the battery is disconnected and the station is returned to the condition you found it before proceeding to the next station. The teacher will inform you of how much time you have at each station. Work quickly and quietly. Record the data during the class period and answer the discussion questions at a later time.

I. Closed Circuits

Station A

1. Materials include a battery, several lengths of wire, and a miniature light bulb.

2. Experiment with different ways to connect the battery, the wires, and the bulb so that the bulb lights.

   In the Results section for Station A, make sketches of the configurations that worked and those that did not. Note details such as the locations where the wires touched the light bulb and which terminal of the battery is connected to a given wire.

3. Disconnect the wires from the battery.

4. Answer Discussion Questions 1-4.

Station B

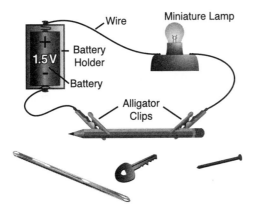

Figure 1

1. Materials include a battery, wires with alligator clips on the free ends, a miniature light bulb in a base, and various objects to be included in the circuit.

2. Attach the wires to the battery terminals as shown in Figure 1.

3. Insert various objects into the circuit by attaching alligator clips to the ends of the objects as shown in Figure 1.

4. Note whether the lamp lights with the object in the circuit. Record whether the object is a conductor or a nonconductor in the Station B data table in the Results section.

5. Remove the object from the clips and disconnect the wires from the battery.

6. Answer Discussion Questions 5-7.

Station C

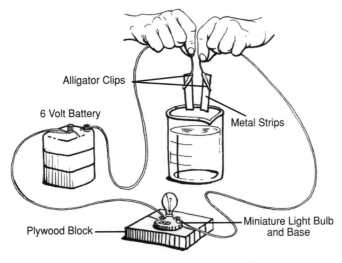

Figure 2

1. Materials include a battery, the conductivity apparatus used in earlier investigations, and three beakers containing distilled water, salt water, and sugar water.

2. Connect the free ends of the wires to the battery. Dip the metal electrodes into the beaker containing distilled water and note if the solution conducts.

3. Rinse the electrodes between each test and determine the conductivity of the other solutions in turn.

4. Disconnect the wires from the battery and rinse the electrodes.

5. Record your observations in the table for Station C in the Results section.

6. Answer Discussion Questions 8-11.

Station D

This station illustrates a simple device called a **galvanoscope.** A galvanoscope indicates the presence of an electrical current by deflecting a magnet. You will alter the amount of current passing through the circuit by adding more batteries to the circuit.

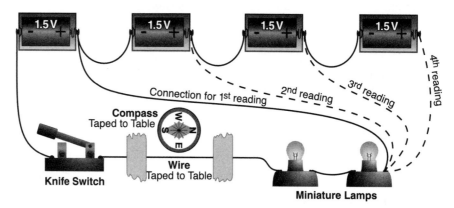

Figure 3

1. Materials include four batteries connected in series or a variable DC power source, a circuit consisting of wires, a switch, several miniature lamps and bases, and a magnetic compass taped to the table.

2. Verify that the switch is open and connect the two free ends of the wires to the first battery. Verify that the compass needle is parallel to the wire next to it. If you are using a transformer, position the control to the $^1/_4$ position (3 V for a 12 V transformer).

3. Shut the switch and observe the needle position (in degrees from north) on the compass. Record your results in the Station D data table in the Results section.

4. Open the switch and connect a second battery in series according to the directions provided by your teacher. The total voltage is the sum of the voltages for the two batteries. If you are using a transformer, move the control to the halfway point.

5. Shut the switch and note the position of the compass. Record your results as before.

6. Repeat steps 2-5 for a third and fourth battery (or the $^3/_4$ and full positions on the transformer).

7. Open the switch and disconnect the wires from the batteries.

8. Complete the graph of voltage versus angle of deflection for Station D in the Results section. You will have to provide the scales for voltage and angle to make the graph as large as possible.

II. Open Circuits

Station E

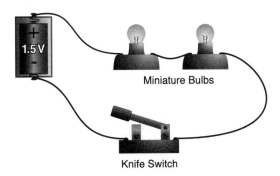

Figure 4

1. Materials include a battery, wires, a switch, and two miniature light bulbs in bases.

2. Verify that the switch is open and connect the free ends of the wires to the battery.

3. Shut the switch and observe that the lamps light.

4. Unscrew and remove one of the lamps and observe what happens. Reinstall the lamp and verify that the lamps light again.

5. Open the switch and disconnect the wires from the battery.

6. Answer Discussion Question 12.

III. Short Circuits

Station F

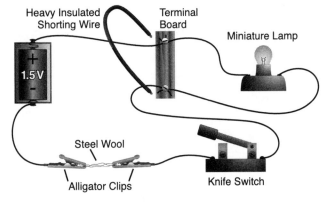

Figure 5

1. Materials include a battery, a circuit consisting of wires, a terminal board with two screws, a miniature light bulb in a base, and two alligator clips with some steel wool between them.

2. Verify that the switch is open and connect the free ends of the wires to the battery.

3. If not already done, pull a few strands of steel wool from the pad and insert them into the circuit between the two alligator clips.

4. Shut the switch and observe that the bulb lights.

5. Touch the two ends of the piece of heavy insulated wire to the screws at points A and B in Figure 5. Record what happens to the lamp and the steel wool under Station F of the Results section.

6. Open the switch and disconnect the wires from the battery.

7. Answer Discussion Questions 13-15.

Station G

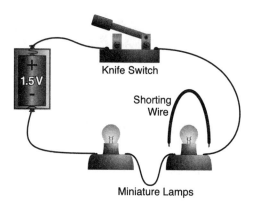

Knife Switch

Shorting Wire

Miniature Lamps

Figure 6

1. Materials include a battery, a circuit consisting of wires, two miniature lamps connected to a switch, and an additional insulated wire.

2. Verify that the switch is open and connect the free ends of the wires to the battery.

3. Shut the switch and observe that the bulbs light.

4. Touch the two ends of the heavy insulated wire to both terminals of one of the lamp bases as in Figure 6.

5. Describe what happened to *both* lamps under Station G in the Results section.

6. Open the switch and disconnect the wires from the battery.

7. Answer Discussion Questions 16 and 17.

IV. Types of Circuits (Optional)

Station H (Series Circuit)

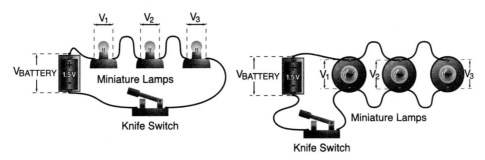

Figure 7   **Figure 8**

1. Materials include a battery and a circuit consisting of three miniature lamps connected in a string (series) with a switch. There may be a voltage test meter at this station also. (See Figure 7.)

2. Check that the switch is open and connect the free ends of the wires to the battery.

3. Shut the switch and note that all three lamps are lighted.

4. Unscrew each bulb one at a time, note what happens to all of the lamps, and screw it back in.

5. Take the test leads of a voltmeter and measure the voltage of the battery. Record this value in the blank labeled "$V_{battery}$."

6. Measure the voltage across each lamp by touching the terminals on the lamp bases with the test leads. Record each voltage reading in the blanks labeled "V_1," "V_2," and "V_3," below.

7. Add up the lamp voltages and enter the sum in the blank labeled "$V_{circuit}$," below.

V_1 _____ $V_{battery}$ _____

V_2 _____

V_3 _____ $V_{circuit}$ _____

8. Open the switch and disconnect the wires from the battery.

9. Answer Discussion Questions 18-20.

Station I (Parallel Circuit)

1. Materials include a battery and a circuit consisting of three miniature lamps connected in a ladder arrangement (parallel) with a switch. There may be a voltage test meter at this station also. (See Figure 8, above.)

2. Verify that the switch is open and connect the free ends of the wires to the battery.

3. Shut the switch and note that all three lamps are lighted.

4. Unscrew each bulb one at a time. Note what happens to all of the lamps and screw the bulb back in.

5. Take the test leads of a voltmeter and measure the voltage of the battery. Record this value in the blank labeled "$V_{battery}$."

6. Measure the voltage across each lamp by touching the terminals on the lamp bases with the test leads. Record each voltage reading in the blanks labeled "V_1," "V_2," and "V_3," below.

V_1 _____ $V_{battery}$ _____

V_2 _____

V_3 _____

7. Open the switch and disconnect the wires from the battery.

8. Answer Discussion Questions 21-23.

Results

Station A

Sketch the circuit configurations that you tried when you attempted to light the lamp. Include both those that worked and those that did not.

Station B
Data Table:
Determining Conductivity

Object	Conductor? (Y/N)

Station C
Data Table:
Solution Conductivity

Solution	Conducts? (Y/N)
Distilled Water	
Salt Solution	
Sugar Solution	

Station D

Directions for graph: Determine the maximum voltage used at this station and write the value at the right end of the horizontal scale (Voltage). Subdivide the scale in equal parts starting at 0 V at the left end. Determine the maximum angle of deflection of the compass from the zero point (north) and write this value at the top of the vertical scale (Angle). Subdivide the vertical scale into equal parts starting at 0° at the bottom. Plot the ordered pairs of points (Volts, Degrees) for the readings in the data table below. Connect the points with a smooth curve.

Data Table: Galvanoscope Voltage vs. Deflection Angle

Volts	Deflection

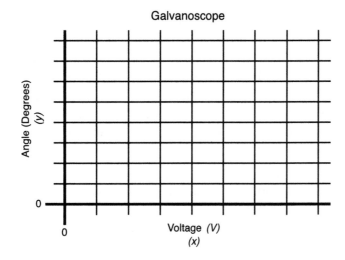

Galvanoscope

Station E

No results are to be recorded.

Station F

Describe your observations when you short out the lamp.

Lamp: _____

Steel Wool: _____

_____

Station G

Describe your observations when you short out one of the lamps.

Shorted Lamp: _____

Nonshorted Lamp: _____

_____

Discussion Questions

Station A

1. What are the three components of a basic electrical circuit? _____

   _____

   _____

   _____

2. What is the function of an electrical load? _____

   _____

3. Considering a lamp as an electrical load, it converts energy from the battery
   into _____ and _____.

4. The electrical path within a light bulb is not always immediately obvious.
   Look at Figure 9. Notice that as with all loads, there is a point where
   charges enter the bulb and a point where they can exit (Diagram A). These
   points are connected by the filament conductor (Diagram B). To ensure that
   no charges bypass the filament, there is an insulating material between the
   contact points on the bulb base. State whether the bulb would light when
   the two wires from the battery are placed at the following pairs of points on
   the bulb in Diagram C:

Contacts	Lights	Stays Dark
W & X		X
X & Y	X	
W & Z	X	
Y & Z		X

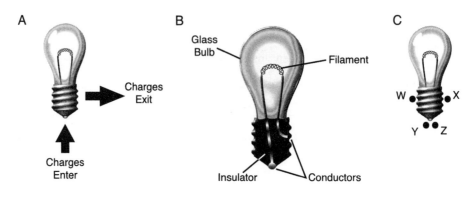

Figure 9

Station B

5. Make a generalization about the conductivity of metals and nonmetals based on your observations at Station B. _____

_____

6. Do the observations you made prove your generalization or merely suggest it? Explain your answer. _____

_____

7. It is believed that the valence electrons of metal atoms are relatively free to move around, giving them the ability to conduct heat and electricity. What could be said about the freedom of valence electrons in nonmetal substances? _____

Station C

8. State whether testing the following resulted in an open or a closed circuit:

   a. Distilled water: _____

   b. Salt solution: _____

   c. Sugar solution: _____

9. What made the one solution conduct while the other two did not? _____

_____

_____

_____

10. In Figure 10, draw arrows indicating the direction the ions will move when the charges shown are applied to the electrodes.

Figure 10

11. When a metal is inserted into a direct current circuit, electrons flow only in one direction—from the negative contact to the positive contact. Considering your answer to question 10, when ions in solution are part of a direct current circuit, how many directions can they move in? _____

_____

Station D

No questions for Station D.

12. Describe why the second lamp went out when the first lamp was unscrewed. _____

_____

Station F

13. When you touched the two screws with the insulated wire, explain what happened to the lamp. Discuss the relative resistance to the flow of charges of the wire and the bulb filament. Which is easier for the charges to flow through? _____

_____

14. Why did the steel wool get hot (and possibly melt)? _____

_____

_____

15. Many years ago when electrical fuses were commonly used in houses, some people replaced a burned out fuse with a penny to restore a circuit, especially if they did not have a replacement fuse. Why was this an unsafe practice? _____

_____

Station G

16. When the first bulb was shorted by the insulated wire, why did it go out?

_____

_____

_____

17. Explain why the second bulb did not go out. _____

_____

_____

Station H (Optional)

18. What happened when each lamp was removed from the circuit? _____

_____

19. How does $V_{battery}$ compare to $V_{circuit}$? _____

20. Make a general statement summarizing the relationship of the energy produced in a circuit and the energy used by the loads in the circuit.

_____

_____

Station I (Optional)

21. What happened when each lamp was removed from the circuit? _____

    _____

22. How does $V_{battery}$ compare to V_1, V_2, and V_3? _____

    _____

23. How did the individual brightness of each lamp compare to the individual brightness of the lamps at Station H? Explain your observation. _____

    _____

    _____

18A INVESTIGATION
Magnetic Fields: Bar Magnets

Objective

The purpose of this exercise is to determine the shape, direction, and strength of the magnetic field around a bar magnet.

Materials

Card stock
Iron filings
Paper
Paper clips
Tape

Equipment

Bar magnets (2)
Lodestone (optional)
Magnetic compasses (5)

Introduction

Magnets can exert a force on certain objects without physically touching them. How these action-at-a-distance forces get from the magnet to an object is an area of intense speculation about the nature of space and matter. Although the process is not understood, the effects of these forces can be described with great precision and their presence can be easily seen by sprinkling iron filings around a magnet. The curved lines formed by the iron filings picture a two-dimensional *cross section* of the three-dimensional **magnetic field** surrounding the magnet. A field is the region of space in which a force acts. A magnetic field is the force field generated by the magnet that will affect another magnet, iron, or any other magnetic material.

These imaginary lines of force are used to visualize the direction and strength of the field, and they have certain properties characteristic of all fields. For example, the closer together the lines are, the stronger the field. Field lines never cross one another. If they did, it would mean that the field points in more than one direction at the point of intersection—a physical impossibility. Magnetic field lines always start at a north magnetic pole and end in a south magnetic pole. Some magnetic field lines ending in a magnet could theoretically originate at an infinite distance away. Practically speaking, though, there are many closer sources of magnetic fields (the earth, power lines, etc.).

Read the entire investigation. Answer the following questions prior to class on a separate sheet of paper. Use complete sentences.

1. How does the magnetic attraction get from the matter in a magnet to an iron nail?

2. Describe a field of force such as an electrostatic or a magnetic field.

3. What is a magnetic field?

4. What determines the strength of a magnetic field?

5. Where do magnetic field lines originate? Where do they end?

6. How will you make the field lines visible in this investigation?

7. How will you determine the direction of the magnetic field?

Procedures

A. Field Strength

If you could count the number of field lines passing through an imaginary plane with an area of 1 cm^2, you could determine the strength of the field. This is not possible, although there exist mathematical methods to calculate field strength. In this investigation, we will use a more physical approach to indicate field strength.

Figure 1

1. Mark a bar magnet every 1 cm from the south pole to the middle. Do the same from the north pole. Label the sections, starting with *A* at the ends and proceeding to the center of the magnet as in Figure 1.

2. Test the strength of the magnetic field at each section, one at a time, by determining how many paper clips will hang from that section of the magnet. Hold the magnet with one hand and add the paper clips one at a time with the other until no more can be supported by the magnet.

3. Enter these numbers in the data table in the Field Strength section of the Results.

B. Field Direction

The direction of any field is indicated by arrows drawn parallel to the field lines. The direction of the field is completely arbitrary (not determined by some supreme authority). Scientists have agreed that the direction of a magnetic field (the ways the field lines point) is the same direction that the north end of a magnet suspended in the field would point.

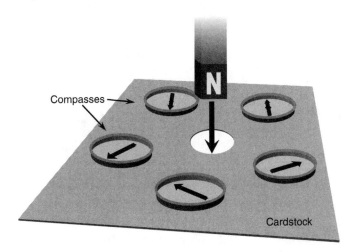

Figure 2

1. Tape the five compasses to a piece of cardstock so that they are equally spaced around a hole just large enough to allow the bar magnet to pass through. (See Figure 2.)

2. Holding the card horizontal, allow the compass needles to come to rest. Slowly pass the magnet vertically down through the hole in the card. Note which pole is entering first and the orientation of the compass needles.

3. Have an assistant finish pulling the magnet through the hole from underneath the card. Note the direction of the compass needles as this process is completed.

4. Draw the orientation of the compass needles when the north end of the magnet is in the hole on Diagram A in the Field Direction section of the Results. After drawing the compass needles, sketch the direction of the field. Follow the same instructions when the magnet is exactly halfway through the hole for Diagram B and when the south end of the magnet is in the hole for Diagram C.

C. Field Lines

We have already discussed the use of field lines to describe the shape of a magnetic field. Recall that field lines are a mental concept or model to help us understand the field theory. Magnetic particles tend to line up parallel to the forces in a field. Your eyes and brain interpret this arrangement of particles as lines.

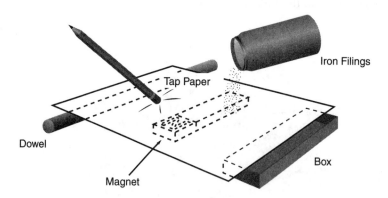

Figure 3

1. Lay one bar magnet flat on the table. Arrange objects around the magnet about the same thickness as the magnet to support the sheet of paper. You can use items such as the top and bottom of the magnet box, wooden dowels, or notebook paper pads. (See Figure 3.)

2. Center the sheet of paper on top of the magnet.

3. Carefully sprinkle the iron filings onto the paper at the location of the magnet. Do not pour the filings in a pile. As more particles are trapped by the field, tap the paper with a pencil to help the particles become oriented with the field. Use enough filings so that all parts of the field can be seen.

4. Sketch the shape of the lines around Diagram A of the single bar magnet in the Field Lines section of the Results.

5. When finished, lift the paper straight up, bend it into a trough, and return the filings to the container.

6. Place two bar magnets so that their opposite poles are in line with each other but separated by about 3 cm.

7. Arrange the paper supports and center the sheet of paper over the gap between the ends of the magnets.

8. Repeat step 3 and sketch the shape of the field on Diagram B. Be sure to label the poles on the diagram.

9. Return the iron filings to the container. Rotate one of the magnets so that two like poles are now close to each other. Replace the paper sheet.

10. Repeat step 3 and sketch the shape of the field on Diagram C. Label the poles on your diagram.

11. Return the filings to the container and clean up any stray particles on the desk.

D. Lodestone (Optional)

Lodestones are natural magnetic ores of iron consisting of a mixture of iron oxides. As with any magnet, lodestones have a north and a south pole.

1. Examine your lodestone sample. Note its shape, color, texture, and relative density.

2. Using a magnetic compass, locate the north and south poles.

3. Sketch your lodestone, including the location of the poles in the designated space in the Results section.

Results

A. Field Strength

Data Table: Field Strength

Section	Number of Paper Clips	
	North End	South End
A		
B		
C		
D		
E		
F		
G		
H		
I		
J		
K		

B. Field Direction

A	B	C
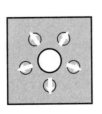	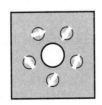	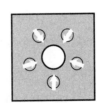
North End	Middle	South End

Magnetic Fields: Bar Magnets

C. Field Lines

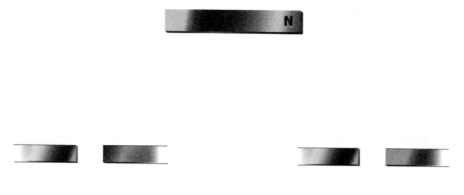

D. Lodestone

Sketch your sample of lodestone in this space.

Discussion Questions

1. Where on a bar magnet is the field strongest? Where is it weakest? _____

_____

_____

2. Does the strength of the magnet taper off gradually, or does it seem to be concentrated at certain locations? _____

_____

_____

3. In what direction does the field point around the north end of the magnet?

_____

In what direction does the field point at the south end? _____

_____

In what direction does the field point in the middle of the magnet? _____

_____

4. (Optional) Is there any external indication of the location of the poles on a lodestone? Explain. _____

_____

Name _____

Date_____ Hour_____

5. How do the fields interact between opposite poles? _____

_____

How do the fields interact between like poles? _____

_____

6. State two ways that the drawings of field lines on a flat piece of paper misrepresent an actual magnetic field.

a. _____

b. _____

Objectives

The purpose of this exercise is to

1. Review the principles of electromagnetism.

2. Investigate the properties of electromagnets.

3. Practice graphing and evaluating data.

Materials

Iron filings
Masking tape
Notebook paper
Wire (insulated), long length (1)
Wire (insulated), short lengths (3)

Equipment

Bar magnets (2)
Batteries, 6 V (3)
Knife switch
Machine bolt
Nails
Rods (glass, plastic, wood)

Introduction

In 1823 William Sturgeon created the first working electromagnet by wrapping wire around a metal bar. No one suspected that these devices would someday guide protons down the path of particle accelerators at nearly the speed of light, hold superheated plasma in invisible containers, or probe the intricate structures of the brain to detect disorders. Today, electromagnets perform all of these functions and more.

You will recall from your textbook that an electromagnet consists of a solenoid (a coil of wire connected to an energy source) surrounding a material that concentrates magnetic lines of force (the core). Some materials are not much better than air at concentrating magnetic lines of force, while others are very effective at concentrating them. Materials that have this property are called *ferromagnetic,* and they tend to make strong electromagnets. In addition to the core material, the strength of an electromagnet depends on the number of wraps (or turns) of the wire around the core as well as the amount of current passing through the wire. Ohm's law states that for constant resistance, the current in a circuit is directly proportional to the voltage applied to the circuit. We will assume that the wire used in this investigation has a small but constant resistance. Therefore, if the voltage is doubled, the current will be doubled.

Pre-Laboratory Questions

Read the entire investigation. Answer the following questions prior to class on a separate sheet of paper. Use complete sentences.

1. Describe the structure of an electromagnet.

2. Give two of the three ways discussed that an electromagnet can be made stronger.

3. Why is it necessary to limit the time that the switch is shut when testing the strength of the electromagnets?

4. What term describes the tiny regions in a ferromagnetic material that give the material its magnetic character?

5. Review the procedure for testing the number of wraps in Part II. If both electromagnets are connected to 6 V batteries, which one will actually have a higher current flow, the one with ten wraps of wire or the one with fifty wraps? Explain.

6. Define *extrapolation* and *interpolation*.

Procedures

I. Domains

The domain theory of magnetism states that ferromagnetic material is composed of very small areas that act like magnets with a north and a south pole (see diagram A in Figure 1). Normally, these areas are not in line, so they cancel each other's magnetic effects (diagram B). However, when placed in a strong magnetic field, these domains become oriented more or less in the same direction, forming a magnet (diagram C).

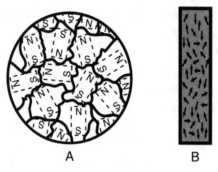

A   B   C

Figure 1

Loose iron filings can illustrate the behavior of domains.

1. Take two bar magnets and lay them side by side with the north poles aligned.

2. Place nonmagnetic spacers around the magnets to support the sheet of paper.

3. Place a piece of notebook paper over the magnets and sprinkle iron filings over the magnets.

4. Note the orientation and concentration of the field lines around the pair of magnets. Sketch your observations around the pair of N–N magnets in the Domains section of the Results.

5. Return the iron filings to the container and turn one of the magnets so that the magnets are in a N–S orientation. Replace the sheet of paper.

6. Again sprinkle the iron filings over the magnets and note the orientation and concentration of the field lines. Sketch your observations around the pair of N–S magnets in the Domains section of the Results.

7. Return the iron filings to the container.

8. Which orientation produced the stronger and more distinct north and south poles? _____

_____

II. Electromagnets

In this part of the investigation, you will construct an electromagnet by wrapping the long insulated wire around the machine bolt, which will act as the core. To make the magnet as efficient as possible, ensure that the wraps are tight and snug against one another. If it is necessary to double the layers of coils, carefully continue the wrapping in the same direction on top of the first layer, working back to the starting point on the bolt.

A. Number of Turns

1. Make an electromagnet by wrapping the long wire around the bolt ten times. Leave about 40 cm free at the end of the wire before you start wrapping. Tape the wire to the bolt to hold it in place. Allow the remaining wire to hang free—do not cut it off.

2. Connect one end of the wire to the 6 V battery and the other end to the switch. Check that the switch is open and connect a short piece of wire from the switch to the other terminal on the battery.

Note: You may be using batteries with a voltage other than 6 V. The procedures may be followed as written for any voltage battery.

3. Scoop the nails into a pile.

Perform the next step as quickly as possible. Remember that while the switch is shut, there is essentially a short circuit through the electromagnet coil since there is very little resistance in the wire. The battery will drain rapidly, and the wire will heat up. Open the switch as soon as the maximum number of nails can be picked up.

4. Shut the switch to energize the electromagnet and pick up as many nails as possible. Select an open area and open the switch to drop the nails so that they can be counted.

5. Count the nails collected and enter this number in Table 1 for Trial 1, 10 wraps.

Electromagnets

6. Repeat steps 3 and 4 twice more, recording the numbers in Table 1 for Trials 2 and 3.

7. Compute the average for the three trials and enter this value in Table 1.

8. Perform this section (steps 1-7) again with twenty, thirty, forty, and fifty wraps. You do not have to unwrap the previous turns; just add the new wraps to the existing electromagnet.

9. In addition to Table 1, record the average results for fifty wraps in the "1 Battery" row of Table 2 and the "Bolt" row of Table 3 in the Results.

B. Voltage

1. Check that the switch is open. Disconnect the wire to the negative terminal of the battery you used in the previous section. Attach one of the short segments of wire to this terminal and connect the other end to the positive terminal of a second 6 V battery. Connect the free wire of the electromagnet to the negative end of the second battery. You now have two 6 V batteries connected in series with a total voltage of 12 V. Enter the total voltage of the batteries used in the "Batteries" column of Table 2.

2. **Perform this step quickly to avoid damaging the batteries and melting the wire insulation.** Scoop the nails into a pile, shut the switch to energize the electromagnet, and pick up as many nails as possible. Open the switch to drop the nails in an open space.

3. Count the nails and enter this number in the "2 Batteries" row of Table 2.

4. (Optional) If available, connect a third 6 V battery in series with the second battery according to step 1 of this section. You now have three batteries in series with a total of 18 V.

5. (Optional) **Observe the precaution of step 2.** Determine how many nails can be picked up at 18 V. Enter this number in the "3 Batteries" row of Table 2.

C. Core Type

1. Without unwrapping the wire, carefully remove the bolt from the fifty-turn solenoid. You may have to rotate the bolt to loosen it from the wire.

2. Disconnect the second and third batteries and reconnect the free wire of the solenoid to the first battery.

3. Scoop the nails into a pile as before. Leaving the core empty, shut the switch to energize the solenoid. Touch the solenoid to the pile of nails and pick up as many nails as possible. Open the switch to drop the nails in an open area and count them. Enter this number in the "Air" row in Table 3.

4. Repeat step 3 for the remaining core types that you were provided. Complete Table 3.

When you are finished, disconnect all wires and set the short lengths aside. Carefully unwrap the bolt and coil the wire according to your teacher's instructions. Return all equipment and materials to their designated locations.

Results

Table 1: Electromagnets and Number of Wraps

Number of Wraps	Number of Nails			
	Trial 1	Trial 2	Trial 3	Average
10				
20				
30				
40				
50				

Table 2: Electromagnets and Voltage

Batteries	Number of Nails
1 (V)	
2 (V)	
3 (V)	

Table 3: Electromagnets and Core Type

Core Type	Number of Nails
Bolt	
Air	
Wood	
Glass	
Plastic	

Discussion Questions

1. State the three variables tested and describe how each variable affected the strength of the electromagnet. _____

_____

_____

_____

2. Plot the data from Table 1 using the number of wraps as the *x* value and the average number of nails as the *y* value. Draw a best-fit line through the resulting points.

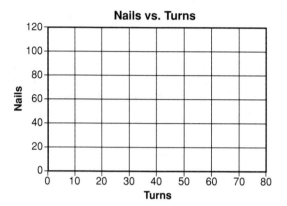

3. Extend the line in the graph from the last datum point to the edge *using a dashed line*. Read the *y* value corresponding to eighty turns on the *x*-axis along this extended line. According to your graph, how many nails could be picked up with eighty turns? _____

Estimating values that are greater than the actual range of data collected is called **extrapolation.** Scientists often obtain information from extrapolations.

  a. What did you have to assume about the shape of the line in order to make your extrapolation? _____

  _____

  b. How accurate would your extrapolation be if your assumption was incorrect? _____

  c. What must scientists ensure when making extrapolations of their data?

  _____

  _____

  d. What are scientists doing when they conclude that a series of similar fossils of increasing complexity in a geologic column are the evolutionary ancestors to a living organism? _____

  _____

4. According to the graph, how many nails could be picked up with thirty-five turns? _____

Estimating values between tested data points is called **interpolation.** Interpolation is a valuable mathematical tool used when one must estimate an unknown value between two known ones.

5. Which do you think would be more accurate, extrapolation or interpolation? Explain. _____

  _____

  _____

6. What is the domain theory of magnets? _____

_____

_____

_____

7. When electrical current passed through the coil, what happened to the domains in the bolt? _____

_____

8. When the switch was opened, what do you think happened to the domains in the bolt? _____

_____

Experimental Evaluation

9. A magnetic field of force can be defined as the strengths and directions of the magnetic forces around the magnet. What is the weakness with this definition? _____

_____

_____

_____

10. Several of the cores did not form an effective electromagnetic field. Do you think this proves that there are no domains in these materials? Explain.

_____

_____

11. Domains are described as theoretical. Why are domains not described as facts or laws? _____

_____

Waves

Objective

The purpose of these demonstrations is to show some of the basic properties of waves.

Introduction

In this demonstration we will be considering some properties of **mechanical waves,** those that travel through a medium. Examples of mechanical waves include water waves, seismic waves, and sound waves. Mechanical waves depend on a disturbance of the particles of the medium to transmit their energy. It was demonstrated by Robert Boyle that sound waves do not travel in a vacuum chamber (a chamber that has had all of the air removed). This is in contrast to light waves, which do not require the presence of any matter for their propagation.

You know that sound waves travel through air, but you also will recognize through practical experiences that sound waves are able to travel through solids as well. The effectiveness of a doctor's stethoscope depends on the fact that sound energy is transmitted better through solids than through air. He cannot hear your heart beating when he is standing next to you. However, when the stethoscope makes physical contact with you, the sound waves are effectively transmitted through the instrument to the doctor's ears. Before the stethoscope was invented, the doctor would place his ear on a patient's chest to help in his diagnosis. When you are underwater, you can still hear garbled sounds that your friend is making even if you can't clearly understand the words. Many marine species use sound waves both as a means to communicate with each other and as sonar to locate prey. Generally the more rigid a substance is, the more effective it is at transmitting sound energy. Water transmits sound better than air, but solids are more effective than water.

Mechanical waves can be classified as either **transverse** or **longitudinal.** Any wave can be fully described by stating its amplitude, wavelength, and frequency. The **amplitude** of the wave refers to the size of the disturbance caused by the source of the wave. The **wavelength** describes the distance between one crest and the next (alternately, it describes the distance from one trough to the next or, in a standing wave, the distance between alternate nodes). The **frequency** of the wave states how many times a complete wave passes a point in one second. The meaning of these terms will become clearer during the demonstrations.

Demonstrations

A. Transverse Waves

1. Observe what happens when one end of the Slinky is rapidly elevated once and brought back down. A one-time event that causes a wavelike disturbance is called a **pulse.** Describe your observations. _____

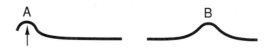

Figure 1

In Figure 1, the arrow below *A* shows that the movement of a particle in the wire is in the upward direction, perpendicular to the length of the wire. However, the movement of the wave itself (the movement of the energy) is parallel to the length of the wire. You can see the "bump" moving along.

2. In diagram B in Figure 1, draw an arrow (labeled "wire") representing the direction that a particle in the wire moved and an arrow (labeled "energy") representing the direction that the energy was originally moving.

3. Draw a picture of the return wave below, labeling the direction of displacement of the wire and the energy flow.

This type of wave is called a **transverse** wave since the particles in the wire are deflected perpendicularly to the path of the energy. Light and some seismic waves are examples of transverse waves. The rebounding of the wave is called a **reflection.** In this case, the reflected wave is a mirror image of the original wave. Notice that although the energy is transmitted down the Slinky, the Slinky returns to its original position after the wave has passed. Mechanical waves require matter to transmit energy, but there is little or no net movement of matter along with the wave itself.

B. Longitudinal Waves

1. Observe what happens when your teacher gathers together a section of the Slinky and then releases it. This is called a compression wave.

2. Describe your observations. _____

_____

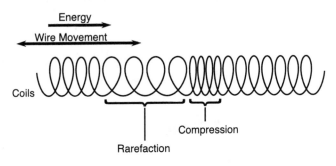

Figure 2

The arrows in Figure 2 indicate the direction of the wire motion and of the energy. This type of wave is called a **longitudinal** wave since the particles are deflected parallel to the same direction as the movement of energy. Sound and some seismic waves are examples of longitudinal waves. Notice in Figure 2 that adjacent to the compression, the particles of matter in the medium are farther apart than in the medium at rest. These regions are called **rarefactions.**

C. Describing Waves

The waves demonstrated thus far are called **pulses** since they were caused by only one vibration. Many waves are generated by an ongoing source of vibrations.

1. Observe as your teacher generates a constant source of transverse vibrations in the wire. You should be able to observe a resulting wave similar to that below. Notice the crest, the trough, the amplitude, and the wavelength. The Greek letter λ (lambda) is used to represent the wavelength.

2. Notice that the amplitude refers to the amount of displacement from the neutral position and is equal to one-half the distance between the top of the crest and the bottom of the trough. The crest and the trough have the same amplitude but in different directions.

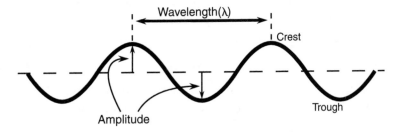

Figure 3

D. Standing Waves

If a constant train of waves moves down the wire and is reflected with the same frequency and amplitude, a **standing wave** develops (see Figure 4 below). Standing waves produce the phenomenon of *resonance*. In a standing wave, the stationary points are called **nodes** and the alternating crests and troughs are called **antinodes.** Standing waves occur not only in wires but also in water and sound waves. Altering the frequency of the wave creates different standing waves.

1. Watch as your teacher alters the frequency of the vibration of the slinky to create different standing waves. What do you notice as the frequency increases? _____

2. How does this affect the wavelength? _____

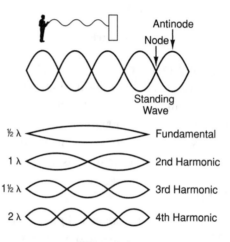

Figure 4

Musical pitches are distinguished by their frequencies. The different standing waves or resonances that are formed by a musical instrument are called its **harmonics** or **overtones.** An instrument produces the fundamental pitch loudest but also produces many overtones at the same time. It is these different combinations of harmonics that give each type of instrument, and indeed each individual instrument, its own unique sound.

E. Wave Speed

1. Notice the speed of a single wave pulse as it moves down the Slinky. Your teacher may ask you to use a stopwatch.

2. Watch as your teacher increases the amplitude of the pulse. Did the greater amplitude change the speed? _____

3. Watch as your teacher sends a train of waves through the Slinky. Did the increased frequency of waves increase the speed of the waves? _____

4. What can be concluded from these observations? _____

   _____

5. What do you think determines the wave speed? _____

   _____

F. Interference

When two waves meet, the resulting wave at any point is the sum of the amplitudes of the two individual waves. This is called **interference.** If two crests meet (or two troughs), the resulting wave will have an amplitude at that point greater than either of the individual waves. This is called **constructive interference.** If a crest and a trough meet, the two waves will offset each other. This is called **destructive interference.** If the crest and trough are of exactly the same amplitude, at the point where they meet, the wave will be cancelled out completely. This principle is used effectively to create high quality headphones for pilots by eliminating virtually all static in radio transmissions.

Your teacher will have two people produce transverse waves on each end of the Slinky according to his directions. Observe and draw the resulting waves at the point where they coincide, labeling the direction of deflection and the direction of the energy flow.

Discussion Questions

1. Define the following terms:

    Wave _____

    _____

    Transverse wave _____

    _____

    Longitudinal wave _____

    _____

    Reflection _____

    _____

    Pulse _____

    _____

    Standing wave _____

    _____

    _____

    Harmonics (overtones) _____

    _____

    Interference _____

    _____

Constructive interference _____

_____

_____

Destructive interference _____

_____

_____

_____

2. Was it proved that all waves that were generated in this demonstration traveled at the same speed in the Slinky? Explain. _____

_____

3. Could you prove that all mechanical waves travel at the same speed through the Slinky? Explain. _____

_____

4. An important aspect of waves is that the medium (Slinky, water, air, vacuum, etc.) determines the speed of the wave and not the amplitude or the frequency. Is this statement a proven fact, a statement supported by many observations, or a guess? Explain. _____

_____

19B TEACHER DEMONSTRATION
Properties of Sound

Objective

The purpose of these demonstrations is to illustrate several of the properties of sound waves.

Introduction

Vibrating matter can produce sound waves. As you have learned in this course, sound travels as longitudinal waves. When a wave hits your eardrum, your middle and inner ear convert that mechanical energy to electrochemical energy. The electrical impulses are transmitted to your brain, where they are interpreted as sound. Sound waves can illustrate properties that are common to all kinds of waves.

Pre-Laboratory Questions

Read the entire demonstration. Answer the following questions prior to class on a separate sheet of paper. Use complete sentences.

1. What equation can you use to calculate the speed of a sound wave, given its frequency and wavelength?

2. What phenomenon causes the change of the perceived pitch of a sound source moving relative to the hearer?

3. Which medium transmits sound energy better, water or air, and why?

4. What instrument will your teacher use to demonstrate the reflection of sound waves?

5. What is the bending of waves around a corner called?

Procedures

A. Pitch, Wavelength, and Frequency

Recall that the speed of a sound wave in any medium is constant for that medium. The speed $(\frac{meters}{second})$ = frequency $(\frac{cycles}{second})$ × wavelength $(\frac{meters}{cycle})$. As a formula, $v = f\lambda$. If v is to stay constant, as the frequency increases the wavelength must decrease.

1. Watch as your teacher places a ruler so that it extends beyond the edge of the table and then thrums the end to start it vibrating. He will vary the length of the ruler extending beyond the edge as he thrums it.

2. What do you notice about the sound as he continues thrumming it while sliding more of the ruler onto the tabletop (shortening the overhanging portion)? _____

3. If you shorten the length of material that is vibrating by sliding more of the ruler onto the tabletop, you generate shorter wavelengths. Since the speed of sound in air is constant, this results in a higher frequency sound wave. Your brain perceives a sound wave with a higher frequency as a higher pitch. Shortening the length of a vibrating string on a violin by pressing your finger onto the fingerboard generates a higher pitch for the same reason.

B. Sound Transmission

What kind of medium transmits sound the best? A sound wave travels because a disturbance in some particles creates a similar disturbance in the particles directly adjacent to them. Naturally, the closer the relationship of the particles to each other, the more efficiently the disturbance will be transmitted. For the sake of illustration, imagine a room that is full of people who are standing about six inches apart. If someone stepped into the doorway from outside the room and gave the person closest to him a good shove, that person would be displaced and would in turn displace the person next to him. This would create a wave of displacement in the group of people, but the effect would lessen the farther it traveled into the room. Now imagine the same room fully packed with people, with no space between them. The same shove from the doorway would displace a lot more people, and the wave of disturbance would travel farther. A gas contains molecules that are far apart compared to the molecules in a liquid. The molecules in a solid are even more closely associated. This is why solids conduct sound energy much better than liquids or air.

1. Listen as your teacher or a partner taps a pencil eraser on the table. Then place your ear on the table and listen again to the same tapping.

2. Which medium produces a louder, clearer sound (makes a better conductor)?

_____

C. Doppler Effect

Describe the pitch of sound as a fast-moving car approaches you, passes close by, and then recedes from you. _____

_____

_____

If the car is traveling at a constant speed, its engine produces sound waves that are at a constant frequency. The speed of the sound waves emitted by the engine in air is essentially constant. However, due to the motion of the car, the spacing of the waves is closer in front of the moving car than it would be if the car were standing still. In the time that it takes to make a new wave, the car moves forward, shortening the distance between the previous wave and the new wave. As we saw in Section A, a shorter wavelength yields a higher pitch. Similarly, the spacing of the waves is greater directly behind the moving car because the car has moved away from the previous wave in the time it takes to make a new wave. Therefore, the wavelength is longer and the pitch sounds lower than at the sound's source.

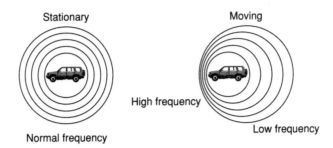

Stationary

Moving

High frequency

Normal frequency

Low frequency

D. Speed of Sound in Air

The speed of a sound wave in air can be calculated by employing the principle of *resonance*. If you direct a pure tone of a single wavelength from a tuning fork into a cylinder, a standing wave will result inside the cylinder. When the standing wave is successfully established, you will hear a distinct increase in the volume of the sound. This resonant condition is established only when the length of the air column in the cylinder is in a specific proportion to the wavelength of the sound. A cylinder with one end closed off will resonate when its length is one-fourth of the wavelength. A cylinder open on both ends resonates when its length is one-half of the wavelength. If you know the frequency and the wavelength of the wave, you can calculate the speed of the wave by using the equation from Section A, $v = f\lambda$. The frequency is marked on the tuning fork, and the wavelength can be calculated by measuring the length of the resonating cylinder.

1. Watch and listen as your teacher demonstrates a resonating cylinder.

2. What did you notice when the resonance was successfully established?

   _____

3. What is the frequency of the tuning fork (Hz)? _____

4. What is the length of the air column in the cylinder (m)? _____

   _____

5. What is the calculated wavelength (m)? _____

   _____

6. What is the calculated speed of sound in air? _____

   _____

E. Forced Vibrations

Sound waves are generated by vibrations, but they can also cause vibrations. If you struck a tuning fork next to a violin string tuned to the same frequency, the string would begin to vibrate as well. If you dampened the tuning fork, the string would continue to sound for a short time. Sources of sound often vibrate at many different frequencies simultaneously. When they cause nearby objects to vibrate that have only certain resonant frequencies, those frequencies become reinforced and can change the perceived quality of the original sound.

1. Listen as your teacher rings a buzzer, first by itself in air and again after bringing it very close to or touching various objects.

2. Describe what happened in the cases where the sound quality changed noticeably. _____

_____

3. Why did this happen? _____

_____

_____

F. Reflection

Sound waves, like all waves, reflect off hard surfaces. This is why echoes occur. A sound source will emit sound waves in all directions simultaneously if the path of the waves is unobstructed. A great increase in loudness can be produced if all of the sound waves can be made to travel in the same direction.

1. Watch and listen as your teacher rings a buzzer, first by itself and then inside of a cone.

2. What do you notice when the mouth of the cone is pointed toward you?

_____

3. Can you explain why this occurs? (Hint: There are two properties of sound illustrated in this example.) _____

_____

_____

4. What do you notice when the mouth of the cone is pointed away from you?

_____

5. Can you explain why this occurs? _____

_____

6. According to your textbook, what is the process called that produces an increase of energy in a sound? _____

G. Diffraction

Do waves travel only in straight lines? If you will think about it, you will realize that sound waves are able to bend around corners. After all, you are able to hear a conversation taking place just around the edge of an open door. This property of all waves is called *diffraction*.

1. Listen as your teacher rings a buzzer, first in the room and then from around a corner.

2. What happened to the sound volume when the buzzer is moved around the corner? _____

3. Why can you still hear the sound? _____

_____

4. Why is the volume of the indirect sound lower? _____

_____

_____

_____

Name _____

Date_____ Hour_____

Wave Properties

Objective

The purpose of this exercise is to demonstrate visually the various properties of all waves.

Introduction

All mechanical and electromagnetic waves exhibit the following properties: straight line propagation, reflection, refraction, diffraction, and interference. **Straight line propagation** means that waves will move in a straight line in a uniform medium. This is the basis for ray theory, which you will study in Section 20C of your textbook. **Reflection** is the rebound of a wave off a barrier. **Refraction** is the bending of waves as they move from one medium to another. It is the result of the different speeds of the waves in the different media. **Diffraction** is the bending of waves as they move around a corner. **Interference** is the interaction of waves as they pass through each other.

These properties can be observed using a device called a ripple tank. A ripple tank is a shallow, typically rectangular, panlike container with a glass bottom. Waves (ripples, actually) are generated by rapidly dipping an object into the water. When a strong light is beamed vertically through the tank, the waves can be projected either onto the ceiling or the floor as alternating light and dark bands. If the light is above the tank, the light area below the tank corresponds to a wave crest and the darker area corresponds to a wave trough. If the light source is below the tank, this pattern is reversed. The reason for this effect is that the curved surface of the wave acts as a lens, either concentrating the light or dispersing it, depending on the direction of light.

Wave generation can include point sources (using a tiny ball or pencil tip) or plane sources (using a bar or ruler). Reflection off a plane surface will be demonstrated by placing a long block in the tank. Refraction will be demonstrated by changing the characteristics of the medium (water depth), and diffraction will be clearly displayed as a wave is observed to bend around an obstruction. The last demonstration will graphically show how destructive interference and constructive interference occur between two wave systems.

Procedures

A. Straight-Line Propagation

In this demonstration, you will observe how waves move, or propagate, through a *uniform medium,* that is, a medium that does not change in character or properties from point to point.

1. Observe as your teacher creates a single pulse in the ripple tank using a small object. This pulse is assumed to originate at a point, so its position is called a *point source.*

   a. All points experiencing displacement associated with a single wave are together called a *wave front.* What is the shape of the wave front associated with a point source? _____

   b. If you followed a single point on the wave front of a point source from the moment it was formed until it hit the side of the tank, what kind of figure would it trace? _____

2. Observe as your teacher now generates a single pulse using a straight bar. The pulse now originates along a linear object, so its starting position is called a *line source.*

   a. What is the shape of the wave front on the long sides of the bar?

   _____

   b. What kind of figure is traced over time by a single point on the wave front? _____

3. State a generalization regarding the path that points on a wave front follow.

   _____

B. Wave Speed

If you performed Investigation 19A, you should have noted that wave speed in a medium seemed to be constant without regard to amplitude or frequency of the wave. In this section you will make observations that will either support or contradict that conclusion.

1. Using a stopwatch, note the time it takes a normal pulse in the ripple tank to travel to the edge of the tank. $t =$ _____

   a. Your teacher will give you the distance the pulse traveled. Calculate the speed of the pulse. $d =$ _____

   $v =$ _____

   b. Your teacher will next produce a single large pulse. Measure the time required for this pulse to reach the edge of the tank and calculate the velocity. $t =$ _____

   $v =$ _____

   c. Observe while your teacher creates a rapid series of pulses simulating a high frequency source. Pick a wave front and determine the time of travel and speed as before. $t =$ _____

   $v =$ _____

2. What can you conclude about the speed of any wave through a given medium? _____

C. Frequency and Wavelength

An essential relationship exists between frequency and wavelength for any wave in a given medium. You know that $v = f\lambda$. Recall that the wavelength of a wave depends on the duration of the original displacement that caused the wave, so λ does not depend on the medium or any other factor associated with the wave (it is an independent variable). Note that since wave velocity is a constant and wavelength is an independent variable, frequency must be dependent on the other two quantities. To show this relationship more clearly, the velocity formula is often rewritten as a frequency formula: $f = \dfrac{v}{\lambda}$.

1. As wavelength increases, frequency _____ .

2. If the wavelength decreases to half the original, the new frequency will be _____ the original.

3. If the wavelength triples, the new frequency will be _____ the original frequency.

4. Mathematically, this relationship is known as a(n) _____ proportion.

5. Observe the ripple tank as your teacher starts with a low-frequency train of waves and slowly increases the frequency. What happens to the wavelength of the ripples? _____

D. Reflection

For this demonstration, your teacher will insert a series of barriers in the ripple tank. Using several wave sources, he will reflect the trains of waves off the barriers at various angles.

1. Describe the pattern of the reflected waves when the source is parallel to the reflecting surface. _____

_____

2. With the reflecting surface oriented at a 45° angle to the direction of wave travel, describe the orientation of the reflected wave fronts compared to the original waves. _____
_____ Sketch this observation in the Results section under Reflection, Diagram A.

3. How does the angle of the incoming wave to the barrier compare to the angle of the reflected wave? _____

4. Observe as your teacher generates reflections with a point source. What is the shape of the reflected wave fronts? _____

_____

5. In the Results section under Reflection, Diagram B, sketch the wave fronts resulting from a plane wave reflecting off a circular object.

E. Refraction

It is difficult to show refraction as a wave passes from one medium to another in a ripple tank because the two liquids would have to be in contact, yet separated. Instead, your teacher will simulate the effect that a shoaling bottom (becoming shallower) along a shoreline has on an approaching wave.

1. Observe as your teacher generates a continuous train of waves that move from the normal depth of the tank across the Plexiglas plate.

2. Compare the speed of the waves over the plate to the waves still in the "deeper" water of the tank. _____

_____

3. Compare the wavelengths of the waves over the plate to the waves still in the "deeper" water. _____

_____

4. It appeared that for the waves above the plate, both wavelength and the wave speed changed in the same direction. Does this violate the wave velocity formula? Explain your answer. _____

_____

5. Sketch your observation in the Results section under Refraction.

F. Diffraction

A characteristic of all waves is the ability to undergo diffraction. In fact, diffraction is one of the key differences in behavior between particles and waves. The model of the electron was greatly complicated when it was discovered that this so-called elementary sub-atomic *particle* exhibited the property of diffraction. Diffraction occurs whenever a wave front intersects the edge of a barrier. Part of the wave is reflected, part moves on in the original direction, and some of the energy is deflected as the wave wraps around the edge of the barrier.

1. Observe as your teacher generates a train of wave fronts that intersect a single barrier. Sketch your observations in the Results section under Diffraction, Diagram A.

2. Next observe as a train of waves intersects two barriers placed nearly end-to-end forming a small gap. What is formed on the side of the gap opposite the wave source? _____

3. What kind of wave source does diffraction through a small opening simulate? _____

4. Sketch your observations in the Results section under Diffraction, Diagram B.

5. (Optional) If you imagine the opening in question 3 reduced in size to a point, make a generalization about every point on a wave front. _____

_____

G. Interference

You learned in Chapter 19 that two waves intersecting each other will interfere in some way but will pass through each other unchanged. When two trains of waves are superimposed on each other, the results can be very complex. In the demonstration of interference, on the projection of the ripple tank pattern, you will note bright areas, dark areas, and places that are of intermediate intensity (gray). Recall from Investigation 19A that a standing wave was characterized by nodes (points that did not move) and antinodes (points that alternately were crests or troughs). When two wave trains are superimposed, the bright and dark areas are the antinodes, while the gray areas are the nodes as the two trains interfere constructively and destructively. The diagram below is a typical interference pattern formed by the wave fronts of two point sources.

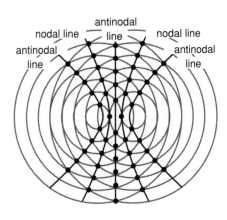

1. Observe the ripple tank projection as two point sources are vibrated to form the interfering wave patterns and note the location of the points of constructive and destructive interference.

2. Note the pattern of the ripples on the surface of the water in the tank. Observe that there are exceptionally high and low points as well as points where the water surface is essentially motionless.

3. Which of the points represent constructive interference? _____

   _____

   _____

4. Explain why some points on the surface of the water appear motionless.

   _____

   _____

Results

A.–C. (No results required)

D.Reflection

A	**B**
Angled Plane Reflection	**Circular Reflection**

E. Refraction

Refraction Across a Plate

F. Diffraction

A

Single-Edge Diffraction

B

Diffraction Through a Gap

G. (No results required)

Name _____

Date _____ Hour _____

Objective

The purpose of this investigation is to

1. Determine the distance of an object and its virtual image from a plane mirror.

2. Determine the relationship between the angle of incidence and the angle of reflection.

Materials

Cardboard
Paper
Tape
Wooden block

Equipment

Plane mirror
Protractor
Straight pins

Introduction

As you have learned from your text, mirrors are capable of generating various types of images depending on the shape of the mirror. Images have several characteristics that have to be evaluated in order to classify them. Before we discuss these, recall that an image is formed in the brain from optical organs (eyes) that must receive and focus incoming light rays. If these light rays arrive in the eyes in the correct angular relationship so that they form a pattern that is recognizable, an image will be formed of an object, whether or not that image really exists in the perceived location. This is the fundamental difference between real images and virtual images. A **real image** can be formed and focused on a surface at a specific location, with or without the presence of a mind to perceive it. A **virtual image** can only be perceived by the mind—it does not really exist.

The reason we see a virtual image is that our eyes and our mind assume that light always travels in a straight line. We know through logic that the light rays forming the image were reflected at the mirror, but our mind perceives the light as coming from behind the mirror. Without logical clues, we could not perceive the difference between a real object and a virtual image. Have you ever been confused by a mirror maze? It is difficult to tell what is real and what is not. Interior decorators use the illusion of virtual images to good effect to make rooms appear larger than they actually are.

Single plane (flat) mirrors can produce only virtual images. These images appear to exist on the opposite side of the mirror from the object forming them. They also appear to be the same size as the object (taking perspective into account), they are upright, and they appear to exist at the same distance from the mirror as the object. Other kinds of images (formed by curved mirrors) can be either virtual or real. They also can have additional properties. They can (1) be formed in front of the mirror, (2) be inverted compared to the object, and (3) appear smaller or larger than the object.

In this exercise you will verify the properties of images formed by plane mirrors using some principles of *ray optics*. One of these principles is that a ray of light will reflect off any polished surface at an angle that is equal to the angle at which it approached the surface. This is called the *law of reflection*. Recall from your text that the angle of incidence and the angle of reflection are measured from the *normal* to the reflective surface.

Pre-Laboratory Questions

Read the entire investigation. Answer the following questions prior to class on a separate sheet of paper. Use complete sentences.

1. What is a virtual image?

2. What is a real image?

3. When you see the reflection of an object in a plane mirror, where does your brain tell you the image of the object is?

4. What is a *normal*?

5. How do you measure the angles of incidence and reflection?

Procedures

A. Virtual Image

1. Draw a line that divides a piece of paper in half and label the line **L.**

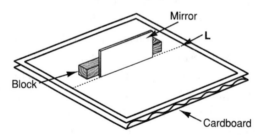

2. Tape the paper onto a piece of cardboard.

3. Use several small pieces of tape to secure a small plane mirror to a wooden block. Place the reflective edge of the mirror on line **L.** (The mirror may be a *front surface* or *rear surface* mirror, which will make a difference as to where the mirror is placed.)

4. Stick a pin into the paper about 3 cm in front of the center of the mirror.

5. Write a small **O** (for Object) by the base of the pin. This will help you to distinguish this pin from the other pins.

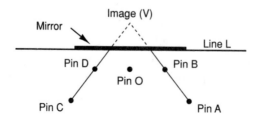

Chapter 20

6. Place another pin about 3 cm in front of and 7-8 cm to the right of pin **O**. Label this pin **A.**

7. With one eye closed, bring your eye down to the level of the cardboard and sight along a line that passes from pin **A** to the reflection of pin **O** in the mirror. Mark this line of sight by placing another pin into the paper at a point between pin **A** and the image of pin **O.** Label this pin **B.**

8. Remove the mirror and pins **A** and **B** from the paper and draw a line through points **A** and **B.** Extend the line 8-10 cm past line **L.**

9. Place the mirror back on line **L.**

10. Place pin **C** about 3 cm in front of and about 7-8 cm to the left of pin **O.** Repeat steps 7 and 8 aligning pin **D** between **C** and the image of pin **O** in the mirror.

11. Remove the mirror and pins **C** and **O.** Draw a line through **C** and **D,** extending it until it intersects line **AB.**

12. The point where lines **AB** and **CD** intersect is the apparent location of the virtual image. Label this point **V.** Draw a line connecting point **O** to **V.** This line should be perpendicular to line **L.** Measure the distance from point **O** to line **L** and from line **L** to **V.** Record these values in Table 1.

B. Angles of Incidence and Reflection

1. Label the points where lines **AB** and **CD** intersect line **L** as points **E** and **F,** respectively.

2. Draw line segments from point **O** to points **E** and **F** to form **OE** and **OF.**

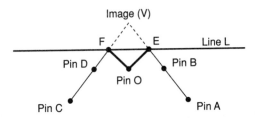

3. Use a protractor to draw a normal (a line perpendicular to line **L**) at points **E** and **F.** Label these lines **EG** and **FH.**

4. Measure the incident and reflected angles: $\angle r_1$, $\angle i_1$, $\angle r_2$, and $\angle i_2$. For example, the incident angle, $\angle i_1$, is $\angle OEG$, while the reflected angle, $\angle r_1$, is $\angle AEG$. Extending the lines with a pencil makes it easier to measure the angles. Record your results in Table 2.

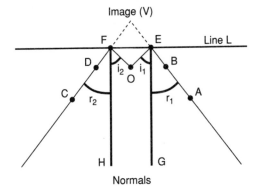

Virtual Images

Results

Table 1: Image Distances

	Distance
Pin **O** to mirror	
Image (**v**) to mirror	

Table 2: Angles

Angle	Measurements
$\angle i_1$	°
$\angle r_1$	°
$\angle i_2$	°
$\angle r_2$	°

Discussion Questions

1. What is the relationship between the distance from the pin to the mirror and its image to the mirror? _____

2. What is the relationship between the angles of incidence and reflection ($\angle i_1$ and $\angle r_1$)? _____

3. If you had used a convex curved mirror, would the angle of incidence and reflection still have been equal? _____

Experimental Evaluation

4. How sure are you that point **V** is the position of the virtual image of pin **O**?
_____

5. How could you improve your confidence for your solution? _____
_____

6. List some sources of error in this investigation. Be specific. _____
_____
_____

20C INVESTIGATION

Lenses

Objective

The purpose of this investigation is to

1. Demonstrate the difference between the terms *focal point* and *image point*.

2. Determine when a convex lens will form real and virtual images.

3. Determine the effect on a real image when the distance between the object and the lens is altered.

Materials

Candle
Matches
Paper
Tape

Equipment

Candle holder
Convex lens
Lens holder
Meter stick
Meter stick supports (2)
Screen
Screen holder

Introduction

Light changes speed as it passes from one medium into another. If the light ray is at any angle other than 90° to the boundary between the media, its direction will change. This bending of light is called **refraction.** The phenomenon of refraction is used principally in optical lenses. There are many different kinds of lenses. In this investigation you will be using a convex lens, one that is thicker in the middle than at the edges.

Before you begin this investigation, some terminology needs to be presented to help you understand the process of forming an image with a lens and the properties of lenses. Some terms are very similar to those used for curved mirrors. The *lens plane* is the imaginary plane passing through the edges of the lens and its optical center. The *principal axis* is an imaginary line perpendicular to the lens plane passing through the optical center of the lens. Lenses are classified by their *focal lengths*. Examine the diagram of the theoretical object in Figure 1. Light rays parallel to the principal axis will converge at a point on the axis called the *principal focus*. The focal length is the distance of the principal focus or *focal point* from the optical center of the lens. Only rays of light originating from an object at an "infinite" distance are mathematically parallel. In reality, no object is infinitely far away or else you would not be able to see it (remember the inverse square law for intensity), but we can use this concept to define the focal length of the lens.

Now examine the diagram of the real object in Figure 1. All real objects are closer than an infinite distance from the lens, so objects will be in focus at locations other than at the focal point. The distance at which the image of a point on an object is in focus is called the *image distance*. For an image to be *in focus,* all rays from any given point on an object intercepted by the lens must converge to a point in the image.

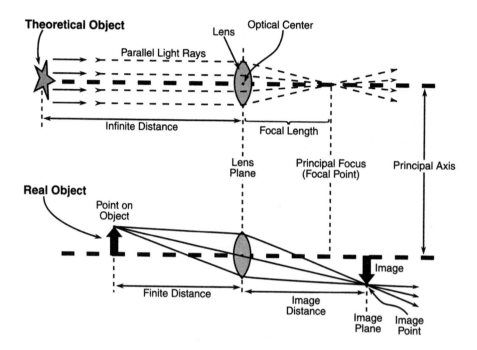

Figure 1

In this investigation you will be using a device called an *optical bench*. It consists of a meter stick supported by two stands and clip-on supports holding a lens, a projection screen, and a light source. Your teacher will explain how to assemble the components. Some questions you should keep in mind during the exercise are

1. What is the focal length of the lens?

2. When an object is placed near the lens so that the light rays striking the lens are not parallel, does the lens form a virtual image or a real image?

3. What is the size of the image in relation to the object?

4. If a real image is formed, what is the image distance?

5. If a real image is formed, is the image right-side up or upside down?

You will see that the answers to these questions depend on the distance between the object and the lens.

Pre-Laboratory Questions

Read the entire investigation. Answer the following questions prior to class on a separate sheet of paper. Use complete sentences.

1. What is refraction?

2. What causes refraction?

3. How can you determine the focal point of a lens?

4. Define the term *image distance.*

5. Would you expect to be able to see an image at any place besides the image distance?

6. Name a device that produces a virtual image that appears larger than the real object.

Procedures

A. Determine the Focal Point of the Lens.

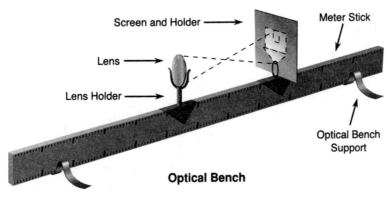

Optical Bench

Figure 2

1. Clean the lens with lens paper or a soft cloth. Insert the lens and the screen into their supports. Set the meter stick into its support legs and clip the screen on top of the meter stick at the 50.0 cm mark. Clip the lens support onto the meter stick between the screen and the zero mark (see Figure 2).

2. Point the meter stick toward a distant object (>10 m away, preferably a brightly lighted object outside the building) and slide the lens along the meter stick until you obtain the sharpest image possible of the object on the screen.

3. Record the positions on the meter stick of the screen and the lens in Table 1. Subtract the lens position from the screen position to obtain the focal length of the lens.

4. Slide the lens support in either direction until the image is no longer in focus. Have different people on your lab team repeat steps 2-3 for two other distant objects.

5. Find the average focal length for your lens.

6. Turn the lens and support around on the meter stick so that the light from the last object is passing through the lens in the opposite direction. Check the focal length again. Do you find any difference? _____

_____

7. Was the image of the object on the screen right-side up or upside down?

_____

8. How did the size of the image compare to the actual size of the object?

_____

Table 1: Focal Length

	Screen Position	Lens Position	Focal Length (mm)
Trial 1	mm	mm	mm
Trial 2	mm	mm	mm
Trial 3	mm	mm	mm
Average			mm

B. Real Images

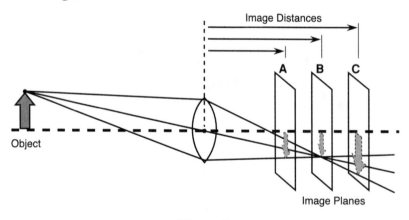

Figure 3

Examine Figure 3. Imagine light rays emitted by the tip of the arrow at the left striking the lens. Three of these rays have been drawn for you. If you assume that the thickness of the lens is negligible, the ray through the center of the lens is not deflected by the lens. The upper and lower rays are called the **limiting rays** because rays farther from the center ray than these fall outside the lens and cannot be focused. The limiting rays are refracted as they pass through the lens and converge (come together). The image of the arrow tip will be in sharpest focus at the point where the rays converge. This is called the *image point*. All points on the object that are a specific distance from the lens will produce an image at the same distance from the lens. These image points are in a single plane called the *image plane* (see Figure 1).

One interesting optical feature should be noted. If the object is not flat but has a lot of depth along the optical axis, not all the points are the same distance from the lens and their images will not all fall on the same image plane.

Chapter 20

Therefore, only part of the image will be in focus. Also notice that light rays will still fall on the screen if it is moved away from the image plane. For a limited distance on either side of the image plane, you can still obtain an image, but it will not be in sharp focus.

Refer to Figure 3 to answer the following questions.

1. Are all light rays coming from the tip of the arrow parallel? _____

2. What rays define the maximum amount of light that can be focused by a lens from any given point on an object? _____

_____

3. At which screen position do the rays from the arrow tip converge to a point? _____

4. What do all of the image points that are in focus form at that position?

_____

C. Image, Image Distance, and Object Distance

The distance 2F, where F is the focal length of the lens, is an important position. You will observe the effect on the image and the image distance as you move the object through this point.

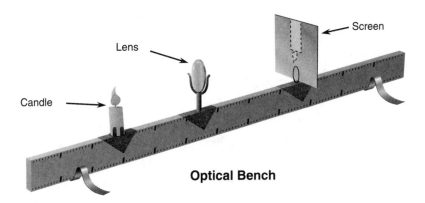

Figure 4

1. Object Distance: 2.5F (typical of a camera lens)

1. From the data you gathered in Section A, calculate 2F for your lens. Use the average focal length calculated by your group.   2F = _____mm

2. Clip the lens in its holder at the 50.0 cm point on the meter stick.

3. Insert a candle into the candle holder and clip it on the meter stick at a distance approximately 2.5F from the lens.   2.5F = _____mm

4. Clip the screen and its holder onto the meter stick on the other side of the lens.

5. Light the candle.

6. Slide the screen along the meter stick until you obtain the sharpest image possible.

7. Note the distance of the screen from the center of the lens. This is D_I, the image distance. Record the image distance in Table 2 in terms of F by dividing D_I by F.

8. Notice whether the image is larger or smaller than the object and whether it is erect (upright) or inverted. Fill in the blanks in the data table for "2.5*F*."

2. Object Distance: 2F (typical of a photocopy machine)

1. Repeat the procedure, placing the candle exactly at 2*F*.

2. Enter the data in the data table.

3. Object Distance: 1.5F

1. Repeat the procedure, placing the candle halfway between *F* and 2*F*.

$$1.5F = \underline{\hspace{2cm}} mm$$

2. Enter the data in the data table.

4. Object Distance: 0.5F (typical of a slide projector)

1. Slide the candle slowly from the 1.5*F* position through the 1*F* position. Move the screen as necessary to keep the image in focus as much as possible. What appears to happen to the image as you approach 1*F*?

_____

2. Repeat the procedure, placing the candle at 0.5*F* from the lens. Slide the screen to obtain the clearest or brightest image possible. (It may be difficult to obtain any image.)

3. **Verifying the Image Type**

   a. Move the lens and its support to the end of the meter stick. Clip the candle at the 0.5*F* distance from the lens.

   b. Move the end of the meter stick to the edge of the table. To best do this step, the candle flame should be easily visible through the middle of the lens from the end of the meter stick.

   c. Close one eye and slowly move your head toward the lens while looking at the candle. Stop when the candle is in sharp focus.

   d. Estimate the distance of the image relative to the position of the lens. Calculate the D_I/F distance and enter it for Image Distance under 0.5*F* (in parentheses).

   e. What is the orientation of the image? _____

   f. How does the image size compare to the actual candle flame? _____

   _____

   g. Where does the image appear to be relative to the lens? _____

   _____

   h. What kind of image is this? _____

4. Enter the data in the data table.

D. Virtual Images: Magnifying Glasses/Binoculars

You have seen that when an object is closer to a convex lens than one focal length, it will form a virtual rather than a real image. In a virtual image, the light rays from the object do not actually converge to a point. This is why a virtual image cannot be projected onto a piece of paper. The image does not exist at any point in space.

1. Magnifying glasses work by fooling your eye into accepting a virtual image that is larger than the real object. Hold the lens close to ($<1F$) the letters on this page. Describe their image size compared to their actual size.

_____

The rays entering your eyes from the magnifying lens make a wider angle than the rays would from the same points of the actual object. Your brain interprets this as the object being closer than it actually is.

2. The image formed in binoculars appears magnified but for a slightly different reason. Binocular objects are always greater than $2F$ away from the lens. In order to produce a useful upright image, the eyepiece is designed so that the pupil of the eye intercepts the outgoing light rays inside the $1F$ distance from the eyepiece. The image is virtual within this distance.

Results

Table 2: Effects of Object Distance

Position of Object	2.5F	2F	1.5F	0.5F
Image distance (D_1/F)				
Type of image (real or virtual)				
Image size (larger/smaller)				
Image orientation (erect/inverted)				

Discussion Questions

1. Explain under what ideal conditions the focal point and focal length are the same as the image point and the image distance. _____

_____

_____

2. Explain how the sun can be used to find the focal point of a convex lens.

_____

_____

3. What happens at the image plane that makes it an important location?

_____

_____

4. Your eye functions as a lens. Which should fall on the retina of your eye, the focal point or the image point? _____

_____

5. Considering your answer to number 4, why is looking directly at the sun dangerous for your eyes? _____

_____

6. Many broad-leaf plants can acquire water burns if they are sprinkled when full sun is falling upon them. Explain how this can be possible. _____

_____

_____

7. Is the image formed on the retina of your eye erect or inverted? _____

_____

8. Is the image formed on the retina of your eye smaller or larger than the object? _____

9. Discuss how different wavelengths of light refract. Give an example.

_____

_____

_____

Material Safety Data Sheet (MSDS)

Chemical _____

1. Hazard index: Health _____   Flammability _____   Reactivity _____
2. Personal protection _____
3. Warnings _____
   Target organs _____
   Storage or disposal instructions _____
4. First aid _____
5. Use _____

Chemical _____

1. Hazard index: Health _____   Flammability _____   Reactivity _____
2. Personal protection _____
3. Warnings _____
   Target organs _____
   Storage or disposal instructions _____
4. First aid _____
5. Use _____

Chemical _____

1. Hazard index: Health _____   Flammability _____   Reactivity _____
2. Personal protection _____
3. Warnings _____
   Target organs _____
   Storage or disposal instructions _____
4. First aid _____
5. Use _____

Chemical _____

1. Hazard index: Health _____   Flammability _____   Reactivity _____
2. Personal protection _____
3. Warnings _____
   Target organs _____
   Storage or disposal instructions _____
4. First aid _____
5. Use _____